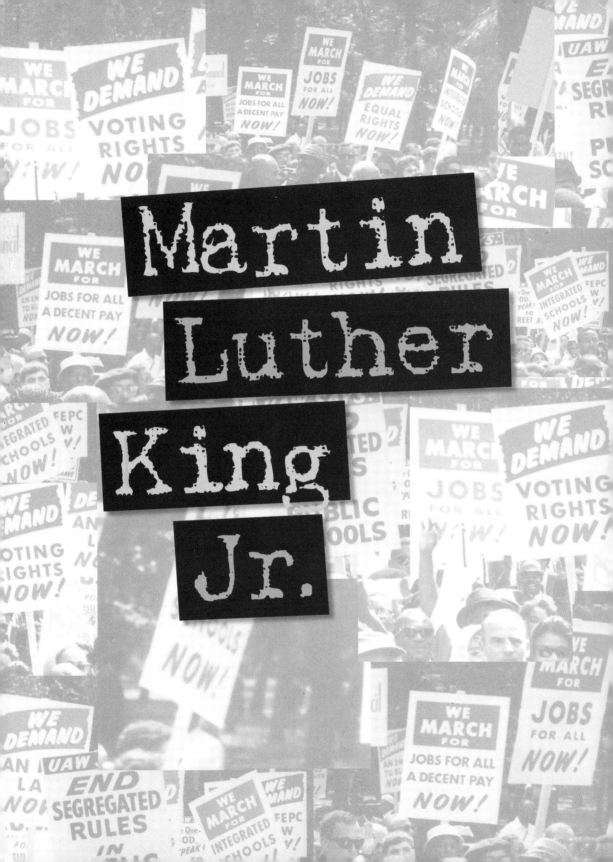

Martin Luther King Jr.

Dreaming of Equality

Ann S. Manheimer

Carolrhoda Books, Inc./Minneapolis

To my parents, Betty and Zola Manheimer, who taught me to cherish freedom, equality, and imagination, and to everyone who struggles for peace and justice

Acknowledgments
My special thanks to Stewart Burns for his invaluable help and support; to David Garrow for his extraordinary insights; to Jeri Chase Ferris, for her keen advice; to Maureen Boyd Biro, Gennifer Choldenko, Lynn Hazen, Anne Isaacs, Kathleen Keeler, Sue Corbett, Margaret Dubois, Karen English, Jane Freeman, Jeanne Miller, Connie Sutton, and Glenys Thomson for their wise comments; to Susan Rose, for making it work; and to Art, Lina, and Allison Swislocki, my first readers, for everything.

Quotations and information from *Testament of Hope: The Essential Writings and Speeches of Martin Luther King, Jr.* reprinted by arrangement with the Estate of Martin Luther King Jr., care of Writers House as agent for the proprietor New York, NY. All Material Copyright Dr. Martin Luther King, Jr. All Material Renewed by the Estate of Martin Luther King Jr.

Carolrhoda Books, Inc.
A division of Lerner Publishing Group
241 First Avenue North
Minneapolis, MN 55401 U.S.A.

Website address: www.carolrhodabooks.com

Library of Congress Cataloging-in-Publication Data

Manheimer, Ann S.
    Martin Luther King, Jr. : dreaming of equality / by Ann S. Manheimer.
        p. cm. — (Trailblazer biography)
    Includes bibliographical references and index.
    ISBN: 1–57505–627–5 (lib. bdg. : alk. paper)
    1. King, Martin Luther, Jr., 1929–1968—Juvenile literature. 2. African Americans—Biography—Juvenile literature. 3. Civil rights workers—United States—Biography—Juvenile literature. 4. Baptists—United States—Clergy—Biography—Juvenile literature. 5. African Americans—Civil rights—History—20th century—Juvenile literature. I. Title. II. Series.
    E185.97.K5M275 2005
    323'.092—dc22   2004002155

Manufactured in the United States of America
1 2 3 4 5 6 – JR – 10 09 08 07 06 05

Contents

Martin Luther King Jr.'s beliefs led him to fight for equality and social justice.

Introduction

Martin Luther King Jr.'s words are known throughout the world: "I have a dream!" Every year on his birthday, recordings ring out the great leader's deep voice pronouncing those famous words.

But King's dream that people not be judged by the color of their skin was not his only dream. He had many. He dreamed of ridding the world of poverty and violence. He dreamed of communities based on love for people instead of love for things.

Those dreams came from many places: his family and friends, people he worked with and people he met while traveling, people from different continents with different religions and of different races. Those many, different people also learned from him, as King's ideas about nonviolence and justice helped to change the world.

Martin Luther King Jr. was born into a system of segregation that separated black people and white people. From an early age, Martin saw that the system was unjust.

1

Remember the Seeds

When Martin Luther King Jr. was little, his father took him downtown to buy shoes. It was the 1930s, and the Kings lived in Atlanta, Georgia. The shoe store was empty. Martin and his father, Daddy King, sat in front. A young white clerk came up.

"I'll be happy to wait on you if you'll just move to those seats in the rear," he said. His words were polite, but he was asking them to move because of their skin color.

"There's nothing wrong with these seats," Daddy King answered. "We're quite comfortable here."

"Sorry," said the clerk, "but you'll have to move."

Daddy King scowled, "We'll either buy shoes sitting here or we won't buy any shoes at all." He stood up, took Martin's hand, and marched him out of the store. As they walked down the street, Daddy King grumbled, "I don't care how long I have to live with this system, I will never accept it."

Atlanta was a big city with strict segregation laws. These Jim Crow laws separated black people and white people, and white people treated black people as if they were inferior. To many people, the experience in the shoe store might have been just another example of segregation. But to young Martin, it planted the seed of an idea.

* * * * *

Daddy King planted many ideas in Martin, ideas that had their roots in his own childhood in rural Georgia. Daddy King's father, Martin's grandfather, had been a sharecropper. Sharecroppers farmed land owned by landlords and only got a share of the crop. When Daddy King was a boy, he overheard the white landlord cheating his father out of money he had earned from cotton seeds. So he prodded his father to remember the cotton seeds.

When the landlord threatened to slap down the boy, Daddy King's father sent Daddy King away. But the boy couldn't keep quiet when something was so wrong. As he left, he called back over his shoulder, "Remember the seeds, Papa."

Daddy King kept those seeds in mind. He left the farm when he was sixteen and walked all the way to Atlanta. There, he worked hard at jobs during the day and hard at studying during the night. Over the next eight years, he graduated from college, became a minister, and fell in love with Alberta Christine Williams.

Alberta's father, the Reverend Adam Daniel Williams, was the pastor of Ebenezer Baptist Church and a leader in the black community's fight for equal rights. His father had been a slave preacher. When Daddy King and Alberta married, they moved into the top floor of Williams's big house on Auburn Avenue and had three children. Christine was born first, in 1928. Martin Luther Jr., born January 15, 1929, was nicknamed M. L. Alfred Daniel, born in 1930, was called A. D.

Martin Luther King Jr., or M. L. as his family called him, was born in this house at 501 Auburn Avenue in Atlanta, Georgia.

The house on Auburn Avenue had a large garden and twelve big rooms. It was surrounded by equally comfortable homes of middle-class black people. Farther up Auburn Avenue, in an area known as Sweet Auburn, were banks, insurance companies, a newspaper, and a radio station, all owned by African Americans. Several black churches were also located on Auburn Avenue, including Ebenezer Baptist.

M. L.'s grandfather, Reverend Williams, died in 1931, and Daddy King took over as pastor of Ebenezer Baptist. Jennie Williams, M. L.'s grandmother, stayed in the Auburn Avenue house with the family. She had a special relationship with M. L. He loved her wonderful spirit and soft heart. When Daddy King—who was both strict and loving—punished M. L. with a whipping, M. L. would refuse to cry. Grandmother Williams cried for him, tears streaming down her face.

M. L.'s home centered on Daddy King. But Daddy King appreciated Mama King's gentle approach to discipline, recognizing that sometimes her kinder way was better. Love was always central in the King household, alongside religion and education.

That love helped give M. L. the strength to deal with segregation's cruelty. Black children growing up in the South then needed a lot of strength. Atlanta, where Martin grew up, was the headquarters of the violent Ku Klux Klan (KKK), a white supremacist organization. White supremacists believed white people were superior, and the KKK used terror to keep white people and black people segregated.

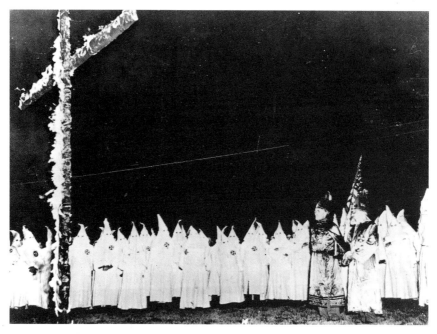

A group of Klansmen burn a cross as a symbol of power during a rally. The Ku Klux Klan used secrecy, intimidation, and violence to preserve segregation and white power in the United States.

Black children were not allowed to swim in public pools with white children. They could not go to school with white children. They could not sit at lunch counters for whites only. They could go to only a couple of movie theaters, which showed only old movies.

As a little boy, M. L. was close friends with the white son of the owner of a store across the street from his home. They had wonderful times playing together until they were old enough to go to school. Then they had to separate—M. L. to the black school, his friend to the white. Suddenly, M. L.'s friend couldn't see him any-more, even outside of school, because, the boy admitted, his family was white and M. L. was colored.

Stunned, M. L. rushed home. His mother took him on her lap and told him the history of black people in America, about slavery and segregation. M. L. decided he would hate all whites, but his parents said it was his Christian duty to love all people. Mama King ended their talk with what black parents in America told their children over and over again—he was just as good as anybody else.

M. L. certainly was as good as anybody else. He was exceptionally bright, good at both schoolwork and sports. His family life revolved around the church, where Daddy King preached, Mama King played the big pipe organ, and Grandmother Williams headed the Missionary Society. Christine, M. L., and A. D. spent Sundays there as well as several weekday afternoons. M. L. enjoyed hearing good

This political illustration from the 1800s shows Africans being sold into slavery during the U.S. slave trade. M. L.'s mother taught him the history of African Americans and U.S. slavery. She also taught him to take pride in himself and in his past.

preachers even before he was old enough to fully under-stand them. After listening to one sermon when he was about ten years old, M. L. said to his father, "That man had some big words, Daddy. When I grow up I'm going to get me some big words."

He made this happen by studying dictionaries and using his new words regularly. His friends weren't put off by his big vocabulary, especially since he usually behaved like other boys. He battled with his brother, once clobbering him on the head with a telephone receiver. He disappeared into the bathroom when it was his turn to do the dishes. And he brawled with neighborhood boys, win-ning many of the fights. But he preferred throwing around big words instead of fists. The other boys were so intimidated that he usually won the war of words too. The seed of another dream was being planted—the idea of victory without violence.

M. L. and his grandmother continued to be close. Once, when he and A. D. were sliding down the banister in their house, A. D. accidentally knocked their grandmother down. M. L. mistakenly thought she'd been killed. He was so upset that he tried to hurt himself by jumping out of a second-story window. Fortunately, the window was not very high, and neither M. L. nor his grandmother was seriously injured.

But when M. L. was twelve years old, he sneaked out without permission to watch a parade on a Sunday. While he was gone, Grandmother Williams died of a heart attack. Grief stricken, he again threw himself out a window. Again, he was not badly hurt—on the outside, at least.

On the inside, he was in terrible pain. His parents comforted him and talked about their belief in the soul's immortality. They said death was a part of life and of God's plan. Another seed was planted.

The King family prospered. Daddy King became a community leader with many business interests. In 1941, when M. L. was twelve, the family moved into a big, yellow brick house, three blocks away.

As M. L. grew, he began to question his strict Baptist upbringing. His Sunday school lessons were fundamentalist—they taught that Bible stories were literally true. M. L. accepted that until he was about twelve years old, when he began to have other ideas.

At the age of thirteen, M. L. skipped a grade and entered Booker T. Washington High School as a tenth grader. He had to take the bus to get to his new school. In those days, Jim Crow laws forced black people to sit in the back of public buses. Even if enough whites didn't get on to fill the front, black people still could not sit there—they had to stand, staring at the empty seats. "I would end up having to go to the back of that bus with my body," M. L. said, "but every time I got on that bus I left my mind up on the front seat. And I said to myself, 'One of these days, I'm going to put my body up there where my mind is.'"

Called to Serve

As a teenager, M. L. loved to roam the neighborhood with his buddies, Rooster, Sack, and Mole. He dressed so well that his friends called him Tweed, for the fine material of his clothing. He flirted with girls and was good at mimicking people. Even though, at five feet seven inches, he was not tall, he was one of the best basketball players around. In high school, he earned only average grades.

But there was a serious side to M. L. When he was fourteen, he won the chance to compete in a state speech contest in Dublin, Georgia, about 140 miles from Atlanta. Even as a youth, M. L. argued for equal rights. In his speech, he said: "Black America still wears chains. The finest Negro is at the mercy of the meanest white man."

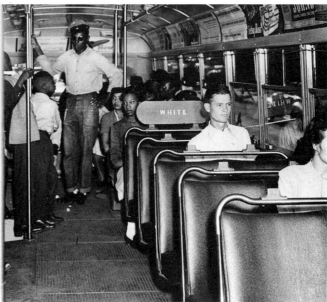

Like the African American man (in cap) in this photograph, M. L. and his classmates had to stand in the crowded black section of a bus during a long class trip. Jim Crow laws made it illegal for African Americans to take seats in white sections, even if seats were empty.

He did well in the contest. Happy, he and his teacher boarded the bus home. But when white passengers came on, the driver ordered M. L.'s group to stand so the whites could sit, and he cursed the students for not moving quickly enough. The students had to stand for ninety miles, the rest of the trip to Atlanta. The injustice made M. L. angrier than he had ever been before.

After he finished the eleventh grade in 1944, M. L. had the opportunity to apply to college a year early. Dr. Benjamin E. Mays, the president of Morehouse College in Atlanta, knew how hard it was for a young black man to get a good education in the public schools. So Dr. Mays had started a special program that allowed black teenage boys to enroll in Morehouse before they graduated from high school if they could pass special tests. Both Daddy King and Grandfather Williams had gone to Morehouse, and M. L. was expected to go there too. He applied to Morehouse and took the tests.

Before he knew whether he'd passed, M. L. traveled with a group of college students to work on a tobacco farm in Connecticut for the summer. It was his first long trip away from home and his first time away from Jim Crow segregation. He happily wrote home, "After we passed Washington the[re] was no discrimination at all[.] [T]he white people here are very nice. We go to [anyplace] we want to and sit [anywhere] we want to."

Despite the doubts he'd had about religion when he was in Sunday school, M. L. became the leader of the students' religious activities in Connecticut. Every Sunday he spoke about the Bible and led the service. He also sang with a boys' choir that performed on local radio and wrote to his mother about going to church with white people. In August he learned that he had passed the tests and was admitted to Morehouse. He left Connecticut on September 12 and, after a stop in New York, headed to Atlanta.

The train that brought him back home also brought him back to segregation. In the dining car, south of Washington, D.C., the waiter showed M. L. to a seat in the rear. Then he pulled a curtain in front of M. L. so the white passengers would not have to see a black person eating near them. M. L. felt as though a curtain had come down over his selfhood (sense and expression of who a person is).

Martin Luther King Jr. entered Morehouse College at the age of fifteen. He lived at home while he attended the small college, shaded by magnolias, about a mile from his house. His poor education quickly showed—he could not read or write as well as other students his age. It didn't help matters that he put more energy into his social life than into his classwork. Around his friends, Martin was a fancy dresser who loved going to parties and dancing with girls (things that strict Daddy King would not have liked). In class he was quiet and always sat in the back.

But he paid attention to his teachers, especially to Dr. Benjamin E. Mays. Dr. Mays admired the Indian leader Mahatma Gandhi and the way he practiced pacifism—rejecting violence as a way to settle disagreements. Dr. Mays also spoke out against segregation. Martin listened eagerly to Dr. Mays's Tuesday morning lectures and stayed to debate with him afterward. As time went on, Dr. Mays visited Martin in his home. They became good friends.

Since he was the son, grandson, and great-grandson of ministers, everyone—especially Daddy King—expected M. L. to become a preacher. Martin, however, had other ideas. In college he asked hard questions about religion. He thought about becoming a doctor or a lawyer. At the same time, he admired Dr. Mays and his other professors for being both well educated and religious. While he was trying to make up his mind, Martin returned to the Connecticut tobacco farm and again led the religious services. He began to sense an inner urge calling him to serve humanity. That urge led to his decision—he would become a minister.

The news made Daddy King very happy. He wanted M. L. to go right to work at his church, Ebenezer Baptist, but Martin wanted to learn more about religion first. He applied to Crozer Theological Seminary in Chester, Pennsylvania, in 1948. His Morehouse professors wanted to give him high recommendations, but since his grades were poor, they had to talk about his potential instead. As one professor put it, "King is one of those boys who came to realize the value of scholarship late in his college career. His ability exceeds his record."

King applied to Crozer Theological Seminar *(above)* to pursue a degree in ministry in 1948.

Martin was accepted into Crozer, where he finally buckled down to work. Since he was years younger than most of his classmates and since most of the students at Crozer were white, he felt tremendous pressure to prove himself. He insisted on being on time, keeping his clothes immaculate, and always polishing his shoes. He was elected student body president, graduated with the highest grade point average in his class, and received the school's major annual prize for scholarship. His professors encouraged him to continue his graduate studies by getting a Ph.D., very unusual for a black preacher in those days. They had no trouble giving him the highest recommendations. He was called "one of the most brilliant students we have had."

Even though Daddy King still wanted M. L. to work with him at Ebenezer, Martin decided to go to Boston University for his Ph.D. Once he got used to the idea, Daddy King agreed to pay his son's expenses. He also gave M. L. a shiny new green Chevrolet.

Martin did well in Boston, but one professor told him to be more careful and give credit to his sources. Unfortunately, Martin didn't follow his advice carefully. Unnoticed by his professors, Martin turned in many papers with portions copied from other authors.

In Boston, Martin liked to eat lunch at Mrs. Jackson's Western Lunch Box for a taste of the good southern cooking that he missed. While there one day, he confided to a friend from Atlanta that he also missed southern girls. She told him about Coretta Scott, who went to school with her at Boston's New England Conservatory of Music. Coretta came from a hardworking farm family in rural Alabama. Martin called her that night. He said that a mutual friend of theirs had said some wonderful things about her.

Martin picked Coretta up in his green Chevrolet the next day. At first, Coretta thought he looked short and unimpressive, but as he talked, he seemed to grow taller and better looking. They spoke about their plans for the future. At the end of the date, Martin told her about the four things he wanted in a wife: character, intelligence, personality, and beauty. He thought she had them all.

Martin and Coretta went to parties and talked about philosophy, politics, and religion. They fell in love. She agreed to marry him even though at that time it meant giving up her own career as a classical singer. But Daddy King wasn't happy about it—he wanted M. L. to marry a girl from the wealthy west side of Atlanta. He told Coretta that M. L. had dated "some of the finest girls—beautiful girls, intelligent, from fine families. . . . Those girls have a lot to offer."

"I have something to offer, too," Coretta told him.

Martin and Coretta went ahead with their plans, and eventually Daddy King came around. More than three hundred people came to their wedding. Daddy King performed the ceremony under an arch in the garden of the Scotts' home.

The newlyweds still had to finish their studies. They rented an apartment in an old house in Boston. On Thursday nights, when Coretta went to class, Martin would cook highly seasoned pork chops, fried chicken, smothered cabbage, or pigs' feet—soul food.

Since he almost had his Ph.D., Martin had to decide where to work. Again, Daddy King tried to get him to work at Ebenezer, but Martin still had other ideas. He applied to be the minister at Dexter Avenue Baptist Church in Montgomery, Alabama. On his first trip to visit the church, Martin felt welcomed by the congregation and also by a young, outspoken pastor named Ralph Abernathy from Montgomery's First Baptist Church.

Coretta and Martin Luther King Jr. moved from New England back to the South and its system of segregation in 1954.

The people at Dexter liked Martin as much as he liked them. They asked him to be their minister. Saying yes meant living away from Mama and Daddy King and moving back to Jim Crow country. Coretta—Corrie, as Martin called her—did not want to return to what she called "the stifling hood of segregation." At the same time, they both wanted to do something about the problems that segregation created. Even more important, the South was home.

In 1954—the year the U.S. Supreme Court decided that racial segregation in public schools was illegal—Martin and Coretta moved back to the South. Martin said, "We had the feeling that something remarkable was unfolding in the South, and we wanted to be on hand to witness it."

3
Something Big

"Black cows!" "Heifers!" "Apes. . . ! " These were some of the milder insults that racist bus drives hurled at black passengers in the days when Martin and Coretta moved to Montgomery. Unfair rules made it nearly impossible for black people to vote. All-white juries and judges regularly convicted African Americans of crimes they did not commit and wrongly set free white people guilty of crimes against black people. White supremacy and KKK terror were brutal facts of life.

When Martin first arrived in town, he had to work hard to finish the paper for his Ph.D. and start at Dexter Avenue Baptist Church. He woke at five thirty every day, made coffee, shaved, then studied and wrote until nine o'clock, when he went to church. He ministered at meetings, funerals, and marriages. He visited sick people and met other ministers. Two days a week, he wrote sermons. On November 17, 1955, Coretta gave birth to their first child, Yolanda Denise. They called her Yoki. Martin had a new baby, a new academic degree, and a new job. He was a very busy man.

Although he and Coretta did not ride on the public buses regularly, Martin knew about the abuse against African Americans. Every day, drivers, all of whom were white, enforced humiliating Jim Crow laws. African Americans were not allowed to sit in the front—they had to crowd into the back even if front seats were empty. They could not sit across the aisle from whites. An entire row of black people would have to stand—no matter how tired, old, or ill they were—so just one white person could sit.

Some drivers were courteous, but others were cruel. Some would hurl transfer slips or change at black passengers, forcing the passengers to bend down to pick them up. Black people often had to pay in front, then get off and walk around back to reboard. Some drivers pulled away before the passengers could get back on. One driver slammed the door on the leg of a blind black passenger and dragged him some distance before the man could free himself.

African Americans tried to stand up for their rights, often with tragic results. Police killed Hilliard Brooks, a black man who had just returned from military service, when he asked for his fare back because the driver had ordered him off the bus. Police arrested two black children visiting from New Jersey, where they were used to sitting anywhere they wanted, for sitting in the whites-only section on a Montgomery bus. Many other black people were beaten and arrested for refusing to follow—sometimes even for just objecting to—the unjust rules.

On March 2, 1955, a few months after Martin came to town, fifteen-year-old Claudette Colvin refused to give up her seat on the bus. Police dragged her, kicking and screaming, to jail. The black community was so angry when she was found guilty that, for a few days, many people refused to ride the buses. When they began to ride again, they were angrier and more sure of themselves.

On December 1, 1955, a seamstress named Rosa Parks boarded the Cleveland Avenue bus in Montgomery's Court Square. It was a cold Thursday night, and she sat down in the middle row, where African Americans were allowed unless the white seats were full. Several whites boarded at the next stop, filling the front rows, leaving one white man standing. The driver told Mrs. Parks and the people sitting by her to move. When she didn't get up, he told her to "make it light" on herself.

It wouldn't have been hard for Mrs. Parks to stand. She wasn't very old or very tired. "The only tired I was," she said, "was tired of giving in." She told the bus driver no, and stayed seated until two policemen boarded and arrested her. Then she went quietly. Her trial was set for December 5.

E. D. Nixon, a leader in the fight against segregation in Montgomery, rushed to arrange for Mrs. Parks's release. Jo Ann Robinson, a professor at all-black Alabama State College, wrote a leaflet asking black people to protest Mrs. Parks's arrest by boycotting, or staying off, the buses on Monday. Without riders, the bus company

Rosa Parks *(left)*, Claudette Colvin, and others refused to obey Southern segregated busing laws in 1955. The arrests and courage of these women led King and the African American community to take peaceful action against these laws through a boycott of Montgomery, Alabama, buses.

would lose money and be pressured to change. The next morning, Friday, tens of thousands of leaflets went to schools, stores, beauty parlors, beer halls, factories, and barbershops. Practically every black person in Montgomery learned about the bus boycott.

At the urging of his best friend, Ralph Abernathy, Martin hosted a meeting of black ministers the night of Mrs. Parks's arrest. They decided to support the one-day boycott and called a mass meeting for the entire African American community for Monday night. They set up a transportation committee to arrange carpools and taxis.

Ministers announced the boycott at Sunday services. Newspapers and television news carried stories about it. Some reports told of white officials accusing black people of organizing "goon squads" to threaten and frighten riders off the buses. Even though the reports were not true, they scared people away from the buses.

Sunday night, Martin and Coretta kept jumping between the ringing of the telephone and the crying of two-week-old Yoki. They hoped the boycott would work. Maybe half the people who normally rode buses would stay off them. Finally, around midnight, they fell asleep.

But not for long. They rose and dressed before dawn on Monday, December 5. The morning was cold. Rain threatened. Workers, mostly women, were already gathering at the bus stop in front of the Kings' house. It looked as though the boycott would fail. Martin sipped coffee in the kitchen as the clock ticked off the minutes. At 5:30 A.M., the buses were rolling.

Suddenly, Coretta called to Martin. She pointed at the South Jackson bus rumbling by. On weekday mornings, it usually carried a full load of black people going to work. That morning, it was empty! Minutes later, a second empty bus rolled by. Then came a third—also empty.

Martin hurried into his car and drove up and down the city streets. The workers gathered on the corners were not boarding the buses. They were taking taxis, walking, sharing rides, even riding mules and horse-drawn buggies. Hardly anyone—black or white—was on the buses. More people had joined the boycott than anyone dreamed possible.

Arriving at the courthouse the day of Mrs. Parks's trial, Martin had to push through a crowd to get inside. Although Mrs. Parks's lawyer argued eloquently against the segregation law, it took the judge just five minutes to find her guilty.

Later that day, black ministers gathered to plan the mass meeting that evening at Holt Street Baptist Church. They created an organization to continue the successful boycott. They named it the Montgomery Improvement Association (MIA) and asked Martin to be president. They chose him because he was a newcomer—considered to be fair and free of local rivalries—and because his speaking talent had already earned him respect.

His first task was to give a speech at the mass meeting. It usually took him fifteen hours to write a sermon. This time he had twenty minutes. He spent the first five worrying that he couldn't do it. Then he jotted some notes and left without supper.

A friend drove, but the streets around Holt Street Baptist Church were so jammed with traffic that Martin had to walk part way. As he left the car, he said to his friend, "This could turn into something big."

The crowd filled the church aisles, balconies, basement and steps, It spilled into the yard outside and onto the surrounding streets. Thousands of black people had come. Loudspeakers were set up outdoors so everyone could hear.

Martin spoke without his notes. "My friends," his voice rang out, "we are here this evening for serious business." He described the arrest of Rosa Parks. "That's right," voices in the crowd gently called back.

Martin paused. His voice rose a shade. "And you know, my friends," he nearly sang, "there comes a time when people get tired of being trampled over by the iron feet of oppression."

Gentle voices grew into a rising cheer, then exploded into a thunder of shouts, applause, and foot stomping that rocked the church and kept going. When the crowd finally settled down, Martin continued. "And I want to say that we are not here advocating violence." People yelled in agreement.

He talked about the "daybreak of freedom and justice and equality." He told the people not to let themselves be pulled so low as to hate others. Through it all, the crowd called and applauded.

Martin ended his speech saying: "Right here in Montgomery, when the history books are written in the future, somebody will have to say, "There lived a race of people, a *black* people, 'fleecy locks and black complexion,' a people who had the moral courage to stand up for their rights. And thereby they injected a new meaning into the veins of history and civilization."

For a few seconds, people sat in stunned silence. Then they jumped to their feet and shouted. Even members of his own church were amazed. They had never before heard such passion from him.

Abernathy asked the crowd if they wanted to keep the boycott going until white officials agreed to make changes on the buses. Everyone cheered in agreement.

That night was the first time Martin spoke to a crowd as the leader of a protest, and he united the black community

King's speech the night of December 5, 1955, at the Holt Street Baptist Church riveted the crowd and united the black community in support of continuing the bus boycott.

in a tide of moral outrage. His speech thrust him into the public eye. Dr. King could no longer be only a preacher.

Over the next few weeks, the MIA leaders met with white officials from the city and the bus company. The whites refused to make any meaningful changes. Instead, they forced taxis to charge more, so the MIA organized a volunteer carpool.

Weeks passed. People grew weary, but every mass meeting lifted their spirits. So did the words of an elderly woman, Mother Pollard. When offered a ride in a carpool, she insisted on walking, saying, "My feets is tired but my soul is rested."

In January the mayor of Montgomery went on television to announce a new get-tough policy. He said the boycotters wanted more than fairness on the buses—they wanted to end segregation, the South's way of life.

Most African Americans did want Jim Crow laws stopped. But the boycotters only asked for a kinder type of segregation—if the back was full and there were empty seats in front, they wanted to sit. That's what they thought they could win.

Even that modest goal angered white people. Under the new get-tough policy, police broke up groups of black people waiting for rides. They trailed carpool drivers and gave tickets for breaking minor—sometimes imaginary—traffic laws. King was arrested for speeding and locked in a filthy, crowded jail cell. He was frightened and embarrassed, until he recognized a couple of people from the boycott. Soon the prisoners gathered around him, sharing their stories and asking for help. "Fellows," he said, "before I can assist in getting any of you out, I've got to get my ownself out." Everyone laughed.

A crowd gathered outside, worrying the officers. They released King. He went back to the safety of home, but home wasn't so safe anymore. Near midnight the next night, Friday, January 27, the telephone rang as he was falling asleep.

"Listen, . . . we've taken all we want from you," an angry voice seethed at King. "Before next week you'll be sorry you ever came to Montgomery."

King had received many threatening calls since the boycott started, but this one scared him more than the others. Maybe it was the late hour. Maybe it was the shock of going to jail that day. Whatever the reason, he could not fall back asleep. All his fears seemed to hit him at once—he feared for his baby, for Coretta, and for himself.

He made coffee and began to pace. Then he sat in the kitchen, the cup untouched in front of him. He didn't want to lead the boycott anymore. He tried to think of a way to get out of it. He knew he couldn't face it alone. Head in hands, he spoke his fears out loud in prayer.

As soon as King finished speaking, he felt stronger. He seemed to hear an inner voice telling him to stand up for truth and righteousness, and if he did, God would always be with him. His fear dissolved. He knew he could do whatever he had to do.

He also knew he might be killed. The movement for civil rights—which was often called "the movement"—needed to be able to go on without him. At a mass meeting three nights later, he told the crowd that the movement would have happened even if he had never been born—he just happened to be there.

While Martin was speaking, Coretta was at home with a friend and Yoki. Coretta heard a thump on the porch. She rushed to the back of the house with her friend just as an explosion blasted in front, shattering windows. Her friend screamed. Coretta raced to Yoki's bed. The baby was fine.

At the meeting, friends told Martin his house had been bombed, but no one knew whether his family was safe. King told the crowd what had happened and urged everyone to go home. Yet, by the time he arrived at his house, several hundred angry black people had gathered. Police officers were trying to calm them, while the mayor, police commissioner, and fire chief inspected the damage. King had to push through the mob to check on his family.

King calms an angry crowd from the front porch of his Montgomery home following a bomb blast there in January 1956. The bomb was likely set to discourage King and the African American community from continuing their bus boycott and pursuing civil rights. It did not.

The crowd grew bigger, angrier, and more uncontrollable. The commissioner asked King to say a few words. When he appeared and announced that no one was hurt, tempers immediately calmed. He told the people that they had to meet violence with nonviolence. He told them not to worry and to go home. They did.

That night, Dr. King single-handedly prevented a bloody riot. If a riot had happened, the movement might have ended there. Instead, an armed and angry crowd protested without any bloodshed. Showing the power of nonviolence, it was a turning point for the civil rights movement.

Two days later, on February 1, 1956, the MIA filed a lawsuit asking a federal court to declare bus segregation in Montgomery unconstitutional. The MIA was now openly challenging the whole system of segregation.

That night, another bomb rocked Montgomery, this time at the home of civil rights activist E. D. Nixon. The white community, it seemed, did not share the commitment to nonviolence.

A few weeks later, a grand jury charged many of the movement's leaders with breaking an old law forbidding boycotts. Instead of waiting to be arrested, the leaders decided to turn themselves in to officials. A crowd outside the courthouse cheered as the leaders arrived, waving and greeting people.

On Sunday evening, February 26, a New Yorker named Bayard Rustin visited King at his home. Rustin had long believed in nonviolence. He had worked with one of the most famous black leaders in America then, A. Philip Randolph, president of the Brotherhood of Sleeping Car Porters. That night, King and Rustin sat over coffee in King's kitchen and talked for hours about pacifism as a tool for peaceful protest.

The antiboycott trials began on March 19, 1956. King's trial went first. The U.S. government tried to prove that he had started the boycott, but the witnesses said he hadn't. As Gladys Moore testified, "Wasn't no one man started it. We all started it overnight."

Even though the government had very little evidence, the judge found King guilty. His lawyers announced they would appeal, asking a higher court to decide if the decision was right. The appeal would take a year. King was released on bail, when his friends paid money to guarantee that he would return to court. The other trials were put aside until his case was finished.

On May 11, the MIA's lawsuit against bus segregation went to trial. Claudette Colvin, the teenager who had been arrested on a bus before Rosa Parks, told her story. Three other black women and two white officials also testified. A few weeks later, the judges ruled that the MIA was right: Alabama's bus segregation was unconstitutional. It was a huge victory for the movement. But the city appealed the ruling, so the boycott kept going. It had been six months.

On Tuesday, November 13—eleven months into the boycott—crowds packed the local courtroom for another hearing, this time to decide whether it was legal for the MIA to run a carpool. The boycott couldn't last without a carpool. King, sitting with his lawyers, expected the worst.

During a short break, a reporter handed him a piece of paper. It said the U.S. Supreme Court, the highest court in the country, had ruled once and for all that Montgomery's bus segregation laws were unconstitutional. That decision was much more important than the carpool hearing. When the judge declared the MIA carpool illegal, it didn't matter anymore. Bus segregation had to stop.

But the boycott could not stop, not until officials formally delivered the Supreme Court order to the city. Since the MIA carpool had been declared illegal, the boycotters organized a neighborhood carpool with different cars.

That night, people from the KKK drove through Montgomery's black neighborhoods. Hooded and robed KKK members usually sent African Americans into the safety of their homes. But this time, they opened their doors, turned on their porch lights, and watched the procession as though it were a parade. The KKK left quickly.

Victorious, King and other boycott activists ride one of the first desegregated buses in Montgomery, Alabama, on December 21, 1956. The city was ordered to desegregate its buses on December 20.

On Thursday, December 20, 1956, U.S. marshals delivered the order to integrate the buses. Finally, the boycott could end.

At 5:55 A.M. the next day, an empty bus pulled up to the bus stop near Dr. King's house. He stepped on and paid his fare. The driver greeted him with a smile. "I believe you are Reverend King, aren't you?" he said.

"Yes, I am," Martin answered.

"We are glad to have you this morning," the driver said.

Dr. King thanked him and took a seat near the front of the bus. Together with Ralph Abernathy, E. D. Nixon, and Reverend Glenn E. Smiley, a white pacifist minister, he rode an integrated bus through the streets of Montgomery.

It had taken thirteen months—382 days—of meeting, walking, and protesting. But finally, the boycotters had won a victory over segregation.

4

Standing Up without Fear

Peace did not last long. Just before Christmas, two days after the first integrated buses rolled through Montgomery, a shotgun blast shattered Dr. King's front door. No one was hurt. Soon after, though, five white men beat up a black teenage girl waiting alone at a bus stop, and snipers shot at the buses, wounding two riders. In response, the city halted night buses, cutting back the only integrated service in Montgomery. That was exactly what the shooters wanted. Leaflets called for people to run King out of town. They were supposedly signed by fed-up black people, but everyone knew they'd been written by white racists.

Riding in a car with friends, Dr. King said, "If anybody had asked me a year ago to head this movement, I tell you very honestly that I would have run a mile to get away from it." But by this point, so many people had been inspired by the civil rights movement that he felt he no longer had a choice. He could not back out.

King's friend Bayard Rustin was in the car that day. So was one of Rustin's best friends, Stanley Levison, a lawyer and a Jewish activist for black people's rights. King listened thoughtfully as they talked about starting an organization based on the MIA to fight for civil rights beyond Montgomery and throughout the South. They had already discussed the idea with another close friend, Ella Baker. King liked the plan. He promised to contact other southern leaders and call a meeting.

The meeting was scheduled for Thursday, January 10, 1957, at Daddy King's church in Atlanta. Martin and Coretta, along with Ralph Abernathy, were staying at Daddy King's house when a telephone call broke the early morning silence—more bombs had exploded in Montgomery. The Abernathys' home had been hit. Nobody was hurt, but a great deal of property had been destroyed. Ralph and Martin flew to Montgomery, leaving the other ministers and Coretta to lead the meeting. When Martin returned the next day, he was thrilled to learn that the ministers had formed the new civil rights organization. It would be called the Southern Christian Leadership Conference (SCLC).

Things looked bad in Montgomery. After the latest violence, the city canceled all bus service for a while.

African Americans worried that they'd lost all they'd won from the boycott. King felt tired from his travels, worried about the new bombings, and concerned that another long struggle was before him. He was also experiencing guilt, wondering if the movement was creating more problems than it solved for African Americans

A few days later, just before his twenty-eighth birthday, King spoke to a mass meeting in Montgomery. Talking about violence and danger, love and peace, he said he hoped no one would die from the struggle for freedom. Then, his voice thick with emotion, he added, "Certainly I don't want to die. But if anyone has to die, let it be me."

King broke down. He could not go on. He gripped the pulpit and remained frozen. The crowd quieted as other ministers helped him sit down.

The breakdown revealed the pressure King felt. He had hoped for quiet after the boycott's success. Instead, he faced growing challenges. Probably the hardest was criticism from people who had worked on the boycott. Some said he traveled too much and didn't pay enough attention to other people's ideas. Some resented him for getting all the credit.

With that credit, though, came threats. Early Sunday morning, January 27, 1957—one year to the day after King had prayed for God's strength in the kitchen—more bombs went off, this time near his home. Twelve sticks of unexploded dynamite were also found on his front porch, their fuses having burnt out. In his sermon that day, Martin explained how his experience in the kitchen had helped him go on even in the face of death threats. "Since that morning, I can stand up without fear," he said. "Tell

The February 18, 1957, issue of *Time* magazine featured King on its cover and listed him as one of the ten most outstanding U.S. citizens. The feature drew national attention to civil rights issues and the growing civil rights movement in the United States.

Montgomery . . . they can keep bombing and I'm going to stand up to them."

A few days later, police arrested seven white men for the bombings. The explosions stopped. Relieved, King turned his attention to the SCLC. In February the ministers elected King to be its president.

That month, *Time* magazine put Dr. King's picture on its cover, and the *New York Times* ran a major story about him and the bus boycott. Martin thought the publicity would ease some of the bad feelings against him and the movement. But the stories overlooked contributions from other activists, and many of them resented it. Aware of the problem, King talked about the price of fame in a sermon a few months later. He told the congregation he knew that his achievements depended on the help he'd gotten from other people.

Fame also brought advantages, including a chance to go to Africa in early March to attend independence ceremonies for the new nation of Ghana. Martin and Coretta were treated to a whirlwind of fancy receptions and balls. He was glad to see that the new rulers did not have on crowns or robes, but instead the caps and coats they'd worn when they were jailed by the British colonial rulers. He said Ghana's success taught the importance of both fighting for freedom and using nonviolence for that fight.

While King was in Africa, his friends Rustin, Levison, and Baker were busy organizing a demonstration for after his return. On May 17, 1957, the third anniversary of the Supreme Court's decision declaring school segregation illegal, about twenty thousand people filled the steps of the

King makes his first national speech before thousands of people at the Lincoln Memorial in Washington, D.C. In his 1957 speech, he asked the U.S. government to enforce African Americans' right to vote throughout the United States, especially in the South.

Lincoln Memorial in Washington, D.C., to call attention to the civil rights struggle. King, speaking last, riveted the crowd. "Give us the ballot!" he called out in bursts like cannon fire, as he talked about the power of the vote. People took up the cry themselves, calling back, "Give us the ballot!" It was King's first address to a national audience. Reporters proclaimed him the new leader of black America.

The next year was relatively peaceful—no bombs rocked King's home and no major fights sapped his energy—but it was certainly busy. He spent most of his time traveling. During one trip, folksinger Pete Seeger taught him the song, "We Shall Overcome." King kept humming it in the car as he left. The song became an anthem of the civil rights movement as people sang it at rallies and demonstrations.

That fall of 1957, King began writing an advice column for a national magazine for African Americans. He answered questions on everything from civil rights to love affairs.

A minister's wife asked how her handsome husband should discourage women who were attracted to him. In his response, Martin practically admitted that he faced the same thing: "Almost every minister has the problem of confronting women in his congregation whose interests are not entirely spiritual."

The many demands on his time greatly frustrated King. On October 23, 1957, delivering his yearly report to his church, he told the congregation that he had to do so many things that he could not do any of them well. King admitted that he was falling behind in his church duties.

While he was speaking, he was interrupted with the news that Coretta had given birth to their second child, a boy. Everyone in the room cheered. Martin announced the child's name—Martin Luther King III—and then cut short the celebrating to return to business. Church members, who thought he should go to the hospital, realized visiting hours would end before the meeting. They called to arrange a late visit for him.

Busy as he was, King was eager to get the SCLC active. He wanted the group to push for black voter registration. First, however, the SCLC needed someone to take charge of its office full time. At Rustin and Levison's suggestion—and despite his belief that women belonged at home—King hired Ella Baker. But, like many people then, he was uncomfortable with the idea of a female leader. Even though Baker was highly skilled and well qualified, King insisted that she be hired only until somebody else could be found.

King spent much of the spring of 1958 working on his first book. *Stride toward Freedom* was about the bus boycott. Telling the complicated events along with his personal story proved very hard. He told Stanley Levison it was the most difficult job he'd ever encountered. Even though he had help from Rustin and Levison, King wrote some parts carelessly and copied some parts from other writers, as he had in his college days.

King's growing fame also made him more of a target. A few months later, he was in New York autographing copies of *Stride toward Freedom* when a middle-aged black woman stepped out of the crowd. She asked if he was Martin Luther

King. When he said that he was, she plunged a seven-inch, ivory-handled Japanese letter opener into his chest. As she was grabbed and handcuffed, King sat calmly, knife in his chest, saying that everything would be all right.

The attacker was taken to a psychiatric hospital, and King was taken to the emergency room of Harlem Hospital, where surgeons operated on him. The weapon had nearly pierced his aorta, a major artery in the body. Any movement, even a sneeze, could have killed him instantly. Days later, he was well enough to start reading his growing mountain of get-well cards. One from a high school girl in New York said, "I am glad you did not sneeze." King had to agree. The sad incident, he said, showed how a climate of hatred and bitterness leads to senseless violence.

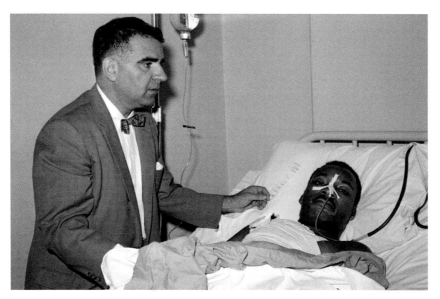

Attended by his doctor, King recovers in a Harlem, New York, hospital following an attempt on his life in September 1958.

Under doctor's orders to relax, King decided to take a trip to India and learn more about Gandhi and nonviolence. He and Coretta flew with friends to Bombay in February 1959. People throughout India recognized them and knew about the bus boycott. The Kings dined with the prime minister, went to press conferences, speeches, meetings, and teas. They met officials, professors, activists, and a student of Gandhi's named Vinoba Bhave. Bhave impressed King with his ideas about landowners giving property to villages and about countries giving up their weapons. Martin called him a saint.

Bhave's ideas—and Gandhi's goals of living simply— had a deep impact on King. He became convinced that many of society's problems came from the desire for material things such as houses and cars. At the same time, he felt pressure to provide those things for his family. He even told Coretta, "a man who dedicates himself to a cause doesn't need a family." Coretta understood his statement as an explanation for why he did not spend more time with his children.

When King came home, he told his congregation what especially impressed him about Gandhi: Gandhi's ability to admit mistakes; his self-discipline, so that his behavior in private was the same as his behavior in public; and his refusal to take for himself any of the money people sent him. Mostly, King wrote, the trip convinced him, "more than ever that nonviolent resistance is the most potent weapon available to oppressed people in their struggle for freedom."

Going to Jail to Help People

On a shining day in April 1959, King addressed a youth march that Randolph, Rustin, and Levison had planned. Speaking to twenty-six thousand black high school and college students in Washington, D.C., he told them to make the fight for civil rights a central part of their lives.

The march caught the interest of J. Edgar Hoover, the director of the Federal Bureau of Investigation (FBI). Hoover believed that members of the Communist Party threatened America. At the youth march, A. Philip Randolph had publicly thanked Stanley Levison. Even though Levison was no longer active in the Communist Party, Hoover decided that Communists were involved in the youth march.

Hoover also believed that Communists were influencing Dr. King. Hoover started to call King, Levison, and the civil rights demonstrations subversive, meaning anti-American, but he was wrong. The demonstrators weren't anti-American—they wanted to make America better.

King decided to move back to Atlanta, where the SCLC had its headquarters. That way, he could work at the SCLC and be copastor with Daddy King at Ebenezer Baptist Church, as the senior King had wanted for so long. Sharing pastoral responsibilities with Daddy King would give him more time. He would still, he hoped, have time for quiet meditation.

The day of his farewell party in Montgomery—February 1, 1960—four black college students in Greensboro, North Carolina, answered King's call for young people to dedicate themselves to civil rights. They sat down in a department store's whites-only lunch counter. The waitress refused to serve them, saying they made their race look bad. Still, they sat there all afternoon and promised to come back. They came back the next day, and nineteen more students joined them. Eighty-five more joined the day after. The following week, the sit-ins spread to other cities and, within two weeks, to other states. Without any help from adults, students were making civil rights a central part of their lives.

As Martin and Coretta moved their young family into the Atlanta house Martin had grown up in, Daddy King reassured his congregation that his son was not coming to cause trouble. But the week after Martin's first sermon at Ebenezer, he flew to North Carolina to tour the lunch counters. Speaking to the demonstrators, he reminded them that their fight was against injustice not white people. He urged them to choose "jail, not bail" to better show their refusal to follow unjust laws.

Student sit-ins spread across the South. Ella Baker called a meeting for the young protesters and helped them organize the Student Nonviolent Coordinating Committee (SNCC, pronounced *snick*). King wanted SNCC to be under the control of adults in the SCLC. But Baker helped the young people keep charge of their organization. The students still wanted King's help, so they asked him and Reverend James M. Lawson, a black minister who had also studied Gandhi, to act as advisers. Excited about the student movement, King called it electrifying and historic.

King meets with student organizers in Atlanta, Georgia, in 1960 to discuss strategies for lunch counter sit-ins. During the sit-ins, African Americans peacefully defied segregation by sitting at whites-only lunch counters. Waves of sit-in protesters were taken to jail.

On May 4, police stopped King for driving with
expired license plates. The officer gave him a ticket. King
paid the fine but did not notice that the judge ordered him
not to break any laws for one year.

It was 1960, and the Democrats and Republicans
would soon hold conventions to decide who would run
for president of the United States. Martin and A. Philip
Randolph agreed that the government needed to pass
stronger civil rights laws. They announced a plan to bring
thousands of protesters to both conventions to demon-
strate that need.

Not everyone liked the idea. New York Congressman
Adam Clayton Powell, who was black, didn't. He threatened to tell everyone that King and Rustin were having a
homosexual relationship unless King canceled the
planned demonstrations. Even though it was a lie, King
was very worried. In those days, being accused of homo-
sexuality would have destroyed his career and made it
impossible for him to continue his work.

King's friends told him that giving in to that kind of
threat was wrong. Still, he worried so much that Rustin
resigned as his special assistant and as director of the
SCLC's New York office. Rustin thought King would
refuse the resignation but, to his disappointment, King
accepted it. Many people thought King's decision
showed a lack of courage. The demonstrations at the conventions went on without Rustin's help, but they were not
very successful.

King went on with his work. On October 19, he joined
thirty-five black students and one white man demanding

King was uncertain. Nash told him the riders wanted to keep going. Farmer urged him to "tell the attorney general that we have been cooling off for 350 years." King agreed and told Kennedy no.

While they were talking, hundreds of angry whites started to riot outside the church. They set fire to a car and surrounded the church, trapping the people at the mass meeting inside.

Late that night, King spoke to Robert Kennedy again. Kennedy sent troops to take the people to safety.

Freedom Riders kept coming. They wanted King to go with them, but he was still on court probation from his traffic violation and could not go without being jailed again. Some people in the movement thought he should join them anyway.

More than three hundred people rode for freedom during the summer of 1961. Many went to prison, where they faced brutal treatment. They kept their spirits strong by singing freedom songs. In September, new rules were issued to make sure people traveling between states would not face discrimination.

New energy from the Freedom Rides gave King reason to be optimistic about the movement against segregation in Albany, Georgia. From December 1961 until the summer of 1962, King gave speeches, led protests, and went to jail to help the Albany campaign. But the city managed to stay segregated anyway. Reporters called the campaign a win for segregation, but King knew segregation was not a "win" for anyone. He tried to learn from the failure so he could help make the next civil rights campaign better.

6

With Audacious Faith

"Segregation now, segregation tomorrow, segregation forever!" Alabama's new governor, George Wallace, pledged when he was sworn into office in January 1963. Birmingham, Alabama, was known as the most segregated city in the country. About ninety miles from the Kings' former home in Montgomery, it was jokingly called Bombingham because so many bombs had exploded at black people's homes, churches, and businesses there. The leader of the fight against racism in Birmingham, Fred Shuttlesworth, wanted the SCLC to help plan demonstrations in his city. Dr. King and his colleagues agreed, even though they knew a protest campaign in Birmingham would be the hardest they'd faced.

The Kings' home situation was not easy, either. Coretta resented Martin's belief that her job was to stay home. Martin tried to be with his family at least for important occasions like birthdays and holidays, but even when he was there, he was often on the telephone. Fortunately, he was home on March 28, 1963, for the birth of their youngest child, Bernice Albertine. Her big brother Marty called her Bunny. Happy as both parents were about their new baby, Coretta was disappointed that she could not go with Martin when he left a week later for the start of the Birmingham campaign.

Demonstrations in Birmingham began April 3. But few people were willing to protest and be arrested. Unfair police behavior usually rallied support, so Martin decided to go to jail again. He was arrested, along with his friend Ralph Abernathy and fifty other marchers, on Friday, April 12. Jailers immediately separated King and threw him into solitary confinement. The twenty-four hours he spent alone there were among the worst in his life: "You will never know the meaning of utter darkness until you have lain in such a dungeon, knowing sunlight is streaming overhead and still seeing only darkness below," he wrote.

Unknown to King, his lawyers told officials in Washington about his treatment. King was moved to a regular cell the next day, but he was still not allowed to call anyone, not even Coretta.

When Easter Sunday arrived without a call from Martin, a worried Coretta began making her own phone calls. One was to President Kennedy. The president called back the next day and assured her Martin was safe. A short

A Birmingham, Alabama, police officer arrests King in April 1963.
While imprisoned, King wrote his "Letter from Birmingham Jail."
The letter expressed an urgent need to end racial oppression.

while later, Martin himself called. They talked about her conversation with the president, the new baby, the press reports, and the food in jail.

Being in jail depressed King. He grew even more depressed when he read in the newspaper that a group of religious leaders said the Birmingham demonstrations had sparked hatred and violence.

He started writing an answer in the margins of a newspaper. He ran out of room, borrowed scraps of paper from another inmate, and kept writing. He borrowed more paper from his lawyer and kept writing.

By the time he finished, Martin had written twenty-two pages. It became known as the "Letter from Birmingham

Jail." In passionate, simple language, the letter outlined his philosophy, methods, and goals. He defended his presence in Birmingham, saying, "Injustice anywhere is a threat to justice everywhere." He explained that demonstrations were needed because people who oppress others will never stop unless they are pressured to stop. He argued that it is a moral duty to disobey an immoral law. He declared that nonviolence was essential because it was wrong to use immoral methods to achieve a moral goal. And he described why black people could not wait patiently for their rights: "When you have seen vicious mobs lynch your mothers and fathers at will and drown your sisters and brothers at whim . . . then you will understand why we find it difficult to wait."

Martin and Ralph were released on bail after nine days in jail. They were disappointed that so few adults were protesting. With such small demonstrations, news reporters were losing interest in the Birmingham campaign. Meanwhile, high school and college students were eager to join the campaign. Even children in elementary school wanted to march. But many adults in the movement did not want to put young people in such dangerous situations, so SCLC and Birmingham civil rights leaders held meetings to decide whether to involve them.

Usually at meetings, King liked to listen to his advisers argue passionately for and against an idea. Then he would summarize what had been said and reach an opinion that could appeal to everyone. This time, he spoke forcefully about the need to recapture the interest of news reporters.

But he could not bring himself to support using young people. He worried that they had not been trained in how to protest nonviolently. He did, however, agree with the suggestion that interested students gather on Thursday, May 2, at Birmingham's Sixteenth Street Baptist Church.

Shortly after noon that day, fifty teenagers walked out of the church, singing and clapping until police arrested them and drove them away. A second group came, then a third, followed by more and more students, marching and singing. The police ran out of paddy wagons and had to use school buses to take them to jail. More than five hundred young people were arrested that day, and more kept demonstrating. Police reacted brutally, attacking the demonstrators with fire hoses, billy clubs, and unleashed attack dogs. Within a few days, Birmingham's jails were completely filled. The events became known as the Children's Crusade.

Most white people wanted the demonstrations to stop. They began talking to the movement leaders. On Friday, May 10, Dr. King and Fred Shuttlesworth, Birmingham's civil rights leader, announced that desegregation would begin and demonstrations would end. Still, the violence did not stop. White people set bombs at black people's homes and businesses. Black people threw bricks and bottles at police. State troopers beat rioters with billy clubs. President Kennedy sent three thousand U.S. troops to the area to put a stop to the chaos. Later that summer, a new Birmingham city council and mayor revoked all of the city's segregation laws. Peace finally won out—at least for the time being.

The events in Birmingham changed the country. Protests swept across the South. The civil rights movement was

Police arrest children and teens during a protest in Birmingham, Alabama. Hundreds of young people were arrested during the protest on May 2, 1963, which was later called the Children's Crusade.

gathering broad appeal. King agreed to take part in a march on Washington planned by his old friends, Bayard Rustin and A. Philip Randolph. They scheduled the march for Wednesday, August 28, 1963. King arrived late Tuesday, his speech unwritten. He started writing a little after midnight, finishing with enough time to get a few hours of sleep while it was being typed and copied.

The next day, about 250,000 people poured into Washington, D.C., twice the number expected. Busloads of people arrived, singing freedom songs. The crowd was supposed to gather at the Washington Monument until the leaders started the march to the Lincoln Memorial. But the people would not wait to be led. Groups started ahead of schedule. The leaders—including Martin—had to rush to catch up for photographs.

King spoke last. He began by reading from his prepared speech. He continued reading until he neared the end. Then he stopped looking at his papers and started speaking from his heart. "I have a dream that one day on the red hills of Georgia, sons of former slaves and sons of former slave-owners will be able to sit down together at the table of brotherhood. . . . I have a dream that one day . . . little black boys and black girls will be able to join hands with little white boys and white girls as sisters and brothers. I have a dream today!"

It wasn't the first time King had used those words, but it was the first time most people heard them. The crowd thundered its approval. Although Martin was unaware of the impact of his speech, President Kennedy recognized it. When King and a group of leaders visited Kennedy

King delivered his famous "I have a dream" speech to more than 250,000 people who rallied for civil rights during the March on Washington on August 28, 1963.

Officials investigate the burned-out Sixteenth Street Baptist Church in 1963. The bomb, set by violent segregationists, killed four young Birmingham girls and enraged the African American community.

after the speech, the president smiled at him and echoed his words, saying, "I have a dream."

Days later, Birmingham exploded again when its schools opened under a U.S. government order to integrate. The worst of the violence was a bomb blast at Sixteenth Street Baptist Church that killed four little girls. Some people, even in the black community, blamed the demonstrators for creating the tensions that led to the killings. King said the bombings resulted from people not doing enough for justice. On Wednesday, September 18, exactly three weeks after the March on Washington, he gave a sermon to eight thousand people attending the funeral of three of the murdered girls. (The family of the fourth girl held a private funeral.)

A couple of months later, the country was stunned when President Kennedy was assassinated. Watching the news reports on TV with Coretta, Martin worried that this was what would also happen to him. Only hours later, the vice president, Lyndon B. Johnson, was sworn in as president of a grief-stricken nation.

On July 2, the movement won a huge victory—passage of the Civil Rights Act of 1964. King stood with some other black leaders for the ceremony as President Johnson signed the law making segregation illegal in public places such as parks, libraries, stores, and restaurants. But King, along with many African Americans, was not entirely

King and other civil rights supporters watch as President Johnson signs the Civil Rights Act of 1964 in July. King believed the law was weak, although it was a major victory for the civil rights movement.

happy about the Civil Rights Act. He believed it did not do enough to protect black people from violence or to protect their voting, housing, and economic rights. He still had plenty to do.

In mid-July, King traveled to Mississippi to help register black people to vote. It was dangerous work. Many black people had been killed in race-related murders, and the Mississippi KKK had threatened to kill King. That summer, SNCC was training and bringing hundreds of mostly white college students from the North to help register black people in the South. Three of the workers—James Chaney, Andrew Goodman, and Michael Schwerner—were murdered. Even though Martin and Coretta knew he might not come back—and even though friends begged him not to go—Martin ignored the danger. He walked door-to-door trying to sign up black people to vote. He toured nightclubs, pool halls, and the area where the three workers had disappeared just before they were killed.

King's schedule was so exhausting that he became ill and, in early October, had to check into a hospital for rest. While he was there, Coretta woke him one morning with a phone call and told him he had won the Nobel Peace Prize. He wondered if he was dreaming.

He wasn't. At thirty-five years old, Martin was the youngest person ever to win the prize, which carried both honor and a fifty-four-thousand-dollar award. Coretta wanted him to keep some of the money for their children's education. Martin insisted on giving it all to civil rights organizations. He believed the award was really for the civil rights movement, not for him individually.

Although good wishes poured in from around the world, only one southern politician, the mayor of Atlanta, sent congratulations. FBI director J. Edgar Hoover, whose dislike of Martin had been increasing ever since the 1959 youth march, said King was more like the "top alley cat" and called him "the most notorious liar in the country."

Hoover was very powerful, and King did not want to get into a fight with him. Publicly, King said that he could not understand why Hoover would say such a thing and that he had sympathy for the FBI director. Privately, King knew Hoover had been wiretapping his telephones (and those of his friends) for quite a while. The wiretaps had picked up embarrassing information about his private life. The FBI had also been spreading rumors that he was a Communist, was dishonest with money, and was having affairs with women. The first two rumors were false, but the last rumor was true.

At the same time, Hoover refused to tell King about threats against his life that the FBI had received. A crude letter arrived at FBI headquarters in December pledging to kill King and other black leaders, as well as Robert Kennedy and President Johnson, for supporting integration. The FBI warned all the people targeted by the letter except King. Fortunately, the writer did not carry out the threats.

The FBI's nasty rumors about Martin threw him into a deep depression. As he knew, even rumors that were not true could damage the civil rights movement terribly.

He was able to hide his depression when he went to Oslo, Norway, in early December to accept the Nobel award. He joked as Coretta and others helped him dress for the formal ceremony. Seven hundred people filled the long, narrow auditorium at Oslo University, which was decorated with thousands of tiny white carnations. The chair of the committee introduced Martin: "an undaunted champion of peace . . . the first person in the western world to have shown us that a struggle can be waged without violence."

Martin swallowed nervously. He began his speech by accepting the award on behalf of the civil rights movement. He talked about nonviolence as the best way to defeat oppression. He said he refused to accept that racism, war, nuclear destruction, hunger, and ignorance were inevitable. He talked about having an "abiding faith in America and an audacious faith in the future of mankind." He ended by accepting the prize on behalf of all people who love peace.

7

We Shall Overcome

Few black people in the South were able to vote in the early 1960s, even though the Fifteenth Amendment to the U.S. Constitution made it illegal to keep people from voting because of their race. Dr. King and the SCLC wanted to focus on voting rights for their next campaign. They decided that Selma, Alabama, would be the best place to do that.

Of the 14,500 black people living in Selma in 1965, only 156 were registered to vote. Threats of violence frightened most away from even trying to register. Those brave enough to try had to face inconvenient hours, unjust poll taxes, difficult applications, and literacy tests that were almost impossible to pass. Even the very few who overcame those obstacles were sometimes rejected. For example, an angry white registrar refused to sign up a black teacher because the teacher could read difficult words that the registrar could not.

The SCLC scheduled a kick-off rally in Selma for January 2, 1965, at Brown Chapel African Methodist Episcopal Church. When Dr. King arrived that day, he saw two young girls, about eight years old, from the nearby housing projects playing outside. He introduced himself and asked them their names. Sheyann and Rachel, they told him. They followed him inside, where he addressed a cheering crowd of seven hundred people: "Our cry to the state of Alabama is a simple one," he said. "Give us the ballot!" Before he left the church, Dr. King told Sheyann and Rachel he hoped to see them the next time he was in Selma.

A few days after Martin returned to Atlanta, Coretta picked up a thin package for him from the SCLC office. Inside, she found a letter and a reel of tape. The letter, whose author claimed to be black, viciously attacked Martin, suggesting he should kill himself. "There is but one way out for you," the caller said. You better take it before your filthy, abnormal fraudulent self is bared to the nation." The tape was an embarrassing sound recording of Martin and other people at drunken parties at hotels during the previous year. Shocked, Coretta called Martin immediately, then did her best to ignore the package.

Martin knew the package was from the FBI, sent on Hoover's orders. The package threw him into even deeper guilt and depression. "They are out to break me," he told a friend over a wiretapped telephone. "They are out to get me, harass me, break my spirit." He said the FBI had no business looking into his private life, and "what I do is only between me and my god."

He told his congregation in Atlanta, "Each of us is two selves. . . . And the great burden of life is to always try to keep that higher self in command." Later, in private, he told a friend—again over a wiretapped phone—that he saw the package as a warning from God that he had not been living up to his responsibilities.

Even though Dr. King made mistakes, he lived up to heavy responsibilities as a world leader. On Monday, January 18, he returned to Selma and led four hundred African Americans on a march to the county courthouse. Protesters marched again the next day, and the next. The jails started to fill with demonstrators. Teachers, undertakers, beauticians, children all marched and went to jail for the right to vote. Still, not one black voter was added to the rolls.

On Monday, February 1, King was arrested at the head of a march of 260 protesters. Over the next couple of days, police arrested about eight hundred schoolchildren for marching. Sympathy for the demonstrators grew as people around the country saw news photos of Martin praying before his arrest and of children being taken to jail.

Even behind bars, Martin kept busy. He wrote letters, notes, and plans. He gave his special assistant, Andrew Young, a list of things to do to keep the campaign alive, such as: "Make personal call to President Johnson urging him to intervene in some way. . . . Consider a night march to the city jail protesting my arrest. . . . Seek to get big name celebrities to come in for moral support."

Good news came soon after Dr. King's arrest. On Thursday, February 4, a federal judge ordered Selma to stop some unfair voting practices, including the literacy test and rejecting applicants because of minor errors. But major obstacles to voting remained. Glad as King was about the court order, he thought it did not go far enough.

King paid bail so he could stay out of jail until his trial. The marchers kept on. Five hundred more were arrested that day. King wrote a letter, which appeared as an advertisement in the *New York Times* the next day: "There are more Negroes in jail with me than there are on the voting roles."

On Tuesday, March 2, 1965, U.S. war planes started dropping bombs on North Vietnam. Since the 1950s, the United States had been helping the South Vietnamese government in a civil war against rebels backed by Communist-led North Vietnam. In a speech that same day, King became one of the first national leaders to call for an end to the Vietnam War when he said, "The war in Vietnam is accomplishing nothing." He told reporters he would write letters to world leaders urging them to talk about peace.

Demonstrations went on in Selma without progress in voting rights. King announced that he would lead a fifty-mile protest march from Selma to the state capital in Montgomery on Sunday, March 7. Governor Wallace said the state would forbid it. The night before the march, Martin's friends asked him not to lead it. They were worried about death threats he had received. Martin knew state troopers would stop the marchers before they left Selma. He also wanted to preach at his own church that Sunday, so he agreed to stay home in Atlanta.

The next day, six hundred peaceful marchers were attacked on the Edmund Pettus Bridge in Selma by hundreds of troopers, some on horseback, wielding billy clubs and hurling tear gas. Sheyann Webb, one of the little girls King had met at Brown Chapel, was there. She knelt to pray with the crowd and then, she said, "a burst of tear gas began. I could see the troopers and policemen swinging their billy clubs. People began to run, and dogs and horses began to trample them. You could hear people screaming and hollering." She escaped to safety, but others were not so lucky. Nearly eighty people had to be treated at the hospital for broken bones, broken teeth, and head gashes. TV showed films of the attack, which soon became known as Bloody Sunday.

King felt agonized by guilt for not being with the marchers during the attack. He called for a second march from Selma the next Tuesday and resolved to lead it. When the marchers reached troopers waiting at the top of the bridge, King called a halt. The fifteen hundred marchers stopped, knelt in prayer, and sang "We Shall Overcome." Then, to almost everyone's surprise, King shouted for the marchers to go back! Confused marchers followed him back to Selma.

Many people in the movement felt betrayed by the turnaround. But King defended it, saying the troopers would have made it impossible to go any farther. He wanted to win the legal right to march to Montgomery without having to fight government troopers.

Days later, white thugs murdered a white minister who had come to Selma to march for civil rights. People all

The nation watched in horror as Alabama state troopers (police) lashed out violently to prevent the civil rights march from Selma to Montgomery on March 7, 1965. The day was called Bloody Sunday.

over the country were stunned. Around the nation, people marched in sympathy with the Selma demonstrators. Congressional members condemned the brutality.

A few days later, on Monday, March 15, 1965, President Johnson introduced a new voting rights law to Congress. Calling Selma a turning point in the "unending search for freedom," he closed his speech with the movement's slogan, saying, "We *shall* overcome." Tears came to King's eyes as he watched. It was the strongest show of support anyone in government had ever given the civil rights movement.

More support came a few days later when a federal judge ruled that Alabama state troopers had no right to stop the demonstrators from marching to Montgomery. President Johnson ordered federal troops to protect the protesters.

This time, with his friends Rabbi Abraham Heschel and diplomat Ralph Bunche, Dr. King led more than three thousand protesters all the way across the Edmund Pettus Bridge on Sunday, March 21, 1965. Angry white racists taunted the protesters but could not drown out the sounds of the freedom songs that rang as the marchers walked past the site of Bloody Sunday.

Led by King and other unwavering leaders, civil rights marchers cross the Edmund Pettus Bridge in Selma, Alabama, on March 21, 1965. They marched on to the state capitol building in Montgomery.

Under a banner carrying the We Shall Overcome motto of the civil rights movement, King speaks at a May 1965 rally in New York. Civil rights activists overcame firm and often violent opposition that year.

King walked most of the fifty miles. Five days later, as they reached Montgomery, the number of marchers swelled to twenty-five thousand. That moment—Martin leading a sea of people, black and white, singing freedom songs as they marched up Dexter Avenue, past his old church—seemed to symbolize how much had changed since the bus boycott ten years earlier.

The Selma protests led to the passage of the Voting Rights Act and capped the struggle against Jim Crow. In the ten short years between the bus boycott and the march to Montgomery, Martin Luther King Jr. and the civil rights movement helped transform the nation. During that time, the United States saw more changes in attitude and law than during any other decade in the country's history.

8
The Flame
of Hope

On August 6, 1965, Dr. King stood with a crowd of white and black leaders in the President's Room of the Capitol Building to watch President Johnson triumphantly sign the Voting Rights Act of 1965. Born in the violence of Selma, King said, the law marked an end of one phase of the civil rights revolution.

Less than a week later, bloody riots broke out in Watts, an inner-city area of Los Angeles, California, where many African Americans lived. Several other northern cities had exploded in violence the year before, but Watts was the worst. The riots lasted for six days, ranged over forty-five square miles, and resulted in four thousand arrests and thirty-four deaths.

Many African Americans had moved North since World War II, while the civil rights movement was focusing on the South. Although they had most of the same legal rights as northern white people, life was segregated anyway. Black people lived in black neighborhoods, often in slums or ghettos. Police were insensitive and sometimes brutal to black people. Unemployment, poverty, and hopelessness plagued the black communities.

King went to Watts. He was shocked at the violence and misery. He had worked to get African Americans the right to eat a hamburger, he commented, "and now I've got to . . . help them get the money to buy it." He sympathized with the rioters—"Violence is the language of the unheard," he said. But he believed their tactics hurt the cause. He felt guilty for failing to get the message of nonviolence across to more black Americans.

Frustrated by slow social change and ongoing discrimination, inner-city residents erupted in anger during the 1965 Watts riots in Los Angeles, California. After the riots, King dedicated himself to bringing nonviolent protest for civil rights and social justice to the entire nation.

That fall, King held an SCLC meeting to discuss putting on a protest campaign in a northern city. His advisers, including his old friends Rustin and Levison, debated the idea. Rustin thought the SCLC didn't have enough resources to fight in both the North and the South. Levison warned that the North was very complex and different from the South. Others wanted to show that nonviolence could work in the North. As usual, King listened quietly to everyone. Then he commented that they could not consider civil rights a national movement if they limited their work to the South. By the close of the meeting, it was agreed that the SCLC would organize protests in Chicago, the country's second-largest city.

While he was focusing on Chicago, King decided to stop speaking against the Vietnam War. Civil rights leaders said he would anger President Johnson and risk losing his support. Government officials accused him of supporting America's enemies. Commentators said he'd let the Nobel Prize go to his head. King said it was hard to fight against the war at the same time he was fighting for civil rights. He asked Coretta to take his place in the peace movement.

To help show the world how bad slum housing was, Martin moved into a rundown apartment in the heart of one of Chicago's ghettos. When the building's owners realized their tenant would be the world-famous civil rights leader, they had it painted and repaired. People joked that the best way for King to improve ghetto housing would be to move from one building to another. Even so, the repairs couldn't hide the grim conditions: the poorly lit entry, the ground-level dirt floor, and the stench of urine.

The refrigerator in King's apartment did not keep food cold, and the heater did not keep the apartment warm.

Coretta stayed in Atlanta with the children for the school year. Martin stayed in Chicago only a few days a week so he could visit his family and conduct Sunday services at his church in Atlanta. Still, he felt the experience was important to teach him about ghetto life. The apartment became a kind of community center.

Neighbors felt their hopes lifted as he visited apartments and shot pool at a local billiard hall so he could meet the community. When he learned about a neighborhood family who wrapped their sick baby in newspaper because they had no blankets or heat, he and his advisers set to work cleaning and repairing apartments. Eventually, the movement won an agreement with managers of several apartment buildings to improve living conditions.

In early June 1966, a shooting pulled Martin's attention back to the South. James Meredith, the first black student admitted to the University of Mississippi, was wounded as he started a protest march from Memphis, Tennessee, to Jackson, Mississippi. King and a group of civil rights workers took up the two-hundred-mile march in his place, along U.S. Highway 51. Over the next few days, the number of marchers swelled to four hundred. Tensions developed as shouts of a new slogan, "Black power!" began to compete with the old rallying cry of "Freedom now!" Although black power meant many different things, people who used it usually accepted violence and taught that black people would be better off living and governing themselves separately from white people.

The slogan troubled King. He thought it divided people and encouraged violence. Although he agreed that black people should be proud of themselves, he thought the black power movement was based on a hopeless belief that America was too evil for African Americans ever to achieve equality. "It claims to be the most revolutionary wing of the social revolution taking place in the United States," he wrote. "Yet it rejects the one thing that keeps the fire of revolutions burning: the ever-present flame of hope."

The march reached Jackson, Mississippi, in July. On the last day, Martin led fifteen thousand people into the state capitol for a final rally. Coretta came, bringing ten-year-old Yoki and eight-year-old Marty for their first march. James Meredith had healed enough to be there too.

Dr. King spoke to the crowd, but he could not hide his unhappiness over the division in the movement. He was disappointed that reporters focused on the black power debate instead of the need for new laws. He worried that people would turn to violence unless the nonviolent movement won some victories.

As soon as the march ended, Coretta and the children moved into Martin's rundown Chicago apartment. The experience, Coretta said, was particularly meaningful for her children, who had never experienced poverty.

On a stifling hot Sunday, July 10, Martin addressed a rally of thirty thousand people at Chicago's Soldier Field. Coretta and all four children sat on the platform, listening to the speeches and the music. Afterward, Martin led a fif-teen-block march to city hall. He and Coretta planned to

King *(center)* leads a civil rights march to city hall in Chicago, Illinois, to protest discrimination and segregation in the city's housing policies.

allow the three older children to go, even though they worried the long walk would tire five-year-old Dexter. But the youngest, three-year-old Bunny, wanted to march too. The great civil rights leader could never resist his youngest child's wishes, so he decided to let her march with them.

It took Bunny barely four blocks to tire out. She rode the rest of the way on the shoulders of Martin's friends and fell asleep before they reached city hall. Once there, Martin taped a long list of demands to the door, calling for better housing, jobs, schools, police, and banks. The next day, Chicago mayor Richard J. Daley said that he agreed with the spirit of the demands and that Chicago was already trying to solve the problems. But he made no concrete promises.

That Tuesday, young people in a slum on the city's West Side tried to cool off by illegally opening a fire hydrant. A riot broke out. King spoke at a mass meeting, like those that had been so successful in the South. He called for peace. But instead of the cheers he was used to, people in the audience sneered and walked out. The riot lasted for two more days until Mayor Daley agreed to King's request to bring sprinklers and portable swimming pools into the neighborhood.

In late July, groups of black and white demonstrators began to hold marches in all-white neighborhoods to protest segregation in Chicago's housing. Angry white hecklers taunted and threw things at the protesters. On Friday, August 5, hundreds of whites surrounded the demonstrators. At first, they jeered. When King arrived, they began to

A stone strikes King in the head during a protest against Chicago's segregated housing on August 5, 1966. An angry crowd jeered and threw things at the demonstrators that day.

throw things. A rock hit him in the head, knocking him to his knees. He was not badly hurt, but the white mob was in a frenzy. The crowd grew into the thousands. It included not just thugs, as had been the case in violent confrontations in the South, but also families. Later, King said he had never before seen so much hate and hostility in a crowd.

Demonstrations continued. Finally, city officials agreed to meet with civil rights leaders. At first, it looked hopeless. The officials wanted the demonstrations stopped before they would make changes, and activists wanted changes made before they would stop demonstrating. When it looked as though the two sides would never agree on anything, King spoke quietly and eloquently: "Let me say that if you are tired of demonstrations, I am tired of demonstrating. I am tired of the threat of death. I want to live. I don't want to be a martyr. . . . I am tired of getting hit, tired of being beaten, tired of going to jail. But the important thing is not how tired I am; the important thing is to get rid of the conditions that lead us to march. . . . This is a great city and it can be a greater city."

His words turned the mood completely around. People at the meeting began to make plans. A week and a half later, after more squabbles and compromises, the civil rights workers and the city officials reached a formal agreement to help stop segregation in housing.

But the ghetto remained bleak nonetheless. Changing laws alone did not end the problems that created the ghetto—these were harder to solve than the problem of segregation. King turned his energy to fighting poverty nationwide and to the war in Vietnam.

9
I May Not Get There with You

"A time comes when silence is betrayal, and that time has come for us in relation to Vietnam." On April 4, 1967, King finally brought the full power of his eloquence to preach against the war. Speaking to a crowd that overflowed New York's Riverside Church, for the first time, he drew the connection between the war and civil rights: "A few years ago there was a shining moment. . . . It seemed as if there was a real promise of hope for the poor—both black and white—through the [government's] poverty program. . . . Then came the buildup in Vietnam and I watched the program broken." He said the country would never spend the money needed to fight poverty so long as it spent money to fight war. He talked about the young black poor being sent to fight and die for liberties they themselves did not have. The United States had to change, he said, "from a 'thing-oriented' society to a 'person-oriented' society."

His speech sparked another storm of criticism, but King felt elated about finally speaking his mind. A week and a half later, on April 15, he helped lead 125,000 people in an antiwar march to the United Nations Plaza in New York. He told them that the promises of President Johnson's antipoverty programs "have been shot down on the battlefields of Vietnam."

King marches with other anti-Vietnam War protesters during the 1967 march to the United Nations in New York City.

The FBI took the speeches very seriously. Hoover told President Johnson that King was being used by people opposed to the government. Martin and his friends noticed the FBI was watching them again—cars trailing them and suspicious sounds on the office telephone. By this time, they knew how to deal with it. They would call each other from phones they knew were not wiretapped. They also made jokes, for example, blaming the FBI for bad telephone connections. Sometimes King laughingly introduced himself to FBI agents who were following him, thanking them for their so-called protection.

The more he thought about Vietnam, the more King thought the civil rights movement needed to change. He wanted to create a powerful new alliance with poor white people. On a television talk show, he described a time he'd been booed by young black separatists in Chicago. He said they were booing the failed hopes he had raised: "I can remember in 1963, when I talked in Washington about my dream . . . some of these very people had great hopes. . . . And yet over and over again, I had to face the terrible experience of seeing my dream turn into a nightmare."

During the summer of 1967, black people rioted in dozens of ghetto areas, leaving eighty-three people dead. Congress rejected a civil rights bill and cut back on programs to fight poverty, even voting down a bill to help poor communities get rid of rats. Some young black militants still jeered at King's nonviolence. At the same time, some whites blamed him for the riots.

Martin grew ever more depressed. Still, he refused to give up. In a television interview, he said, "I feel that we can win this struggle. I have not lost faith in that possibility, and that's the only thing that keeps me going."

That September, attorney Marian Wright, the first black female lawyer in Mississippi, came to Martin's office in Atlanta. She brought with her four unemployed black farmworkers from Mississippi and an idea—to bring poor people from Mississippi, like the men with her, to sit-in at offices in Washington, D.C., until the government took action against unemployment.

King liked the idea, but he wanted to do more. He wanted to bring thousands of poor people from all over the country in waves, demanding jobs or income for everyone. He called it the Poor People's Campaign. At an SCLC meeting on January 15, 1968, he told his staff he wanted the Poor People's Campaign to be as militant and dramatic as a riot, without destroying life or property.

The staff stopped Martin on his way out of the meeting. "Now, some folks celebrate Abraham Lincoln's [birthday]," a friend said, "but we are going to celebrate Martin Luther King Day today. Don't let him out of here!" Martin was all smiles as the staff sang "Happy Birthday" and unofficially celebrated the first Martin Luther King Jr. Day, honoring his thirty-ninth birthday.

In March, in the midst of his work on the Poor People's Campaign, King received a call from an old friend, James Lawson, who had been an adviser to SNCC when it was founded. Lawson asked him to come to Memphis, Tennessee, to talk to black sanitation employees protesting unfair working conditions. Martin agreed. He planned to give a speech and come home right away.

Before leaving, Martin stopped at a florist to send Coretta red carnations. She was thrilled to get them but surprised to find they were artificial. He explained that he wanted to give her something that she could keep.

King's friends predicted that he'd end up doing more than just giving a speech in Memphis. They were right. After delivering a fiery address on Monday, March 18, 1968, he promised to come back soon to lead a mass march.

Impressed by the enthusiastic response to his speech, King was in unusually good spirits when he left Memphis. A couple of days later, he took Marty and Dexter with him to fly around Georgia to sign up volunteers for

In early 1968, King reached out to the poor across the United States to help organize the Poor People's Campaign. Here King greets people in a Newark, New Jersey, neighborhood.

the Poor People's Campaign. He proudly introduced the boys to the crowds all along the way. It was a rare treat for his sons and also for Martin, who felt guilty for seeing so little of them. But airplane engine troubles pulled them behind schedule, and they arrived home in Atlanta late at night and exhausted.

Despite the pleasure of his sons' company, King was downhearted after the tour. People were not volunteering for the Poor People's Campaign. There were undercover FBI agents at meetings, interfering with the campaign's plans. On top of that, the SCLC was running out of money. Martin was so anxious about it all that he had trouble sleeping. When he went on a speaking tour to New York, many of his appearances had to be canceled because he was so tired. He told one reporter he was getting about two hours of sleep a night.

After a late night flight home to Atlanta from New York, King caught an early plane to Memphis for the march he'd promised to lead. He arrived more than an hour late, exhausted and depressed.

Marchers had begun to gather early in the unseasonable heat, the crowd growing bigger and more agitated as the people waited for Dr. King. Teenagers sneaked out of school to join the protest. According to a rumor, police had shot a black girl trying to leave her high school. It wasn't true, but it inflamed emotions. Drunks gathered on street corners nearby, and tempers rose as the crowd waited. By the time King showed up, the protesters numbered twenty thousand. Many were young. Many were angry.

Martin knew as soon as he arrived that the crowd was poorly disciplined. He spoke with the leaders about delaying the march but decided that would cause even more problems. Tired and worried, he started out. After just a few blocks, he heard glass breaking at the rear of the march. Demonstrators were using their protest signs to shatter storefront windows and loot the wares. The disturbance spread. Police came. Residents from nearby housing projects showed up. Rocks, bricks, and tear gas began to fly.

Exhausted and anxious as he already felt, the increasing violence confused and frightened King. He told his friends that he had to get out of there. His friends agreed. With the help of a police escort, Martin's friends drove him to safety.

In the calm of a hotel room, a stunned King wondered aloud at the violence. It was the only time a march he'd led had turned into a riot. He worried it might happen again, in the upcoming Poor People's Campaign. King knew his opponents, such as the FBI, could use the Memphis violence to argue that he would not be able to keep the campaign peaceful. It depressed him terribly. He told his friend Abernathy, "Ralph, we live in a sick nation. . . . Maybe we just have to let violence run its course."

He felt better after speaking with Stanley Levison, who reminded him that most of the marchers were peaceful and that experienced SCLC workers would be able to keep the Poor People's Campaign under control. Still, Martin was so upset he couldn't sleep again that night. He felt he had to prove he could lead a nonviolent march in Memphis before he could go ahead with the Poor People's Campaign.

King marches with other protesters during the 1968 sanitation workers' strike in Memphis, Tennessee. To King's dismay and frustration, the protest ended in violence when some demonstrators rioted.

Most people believed a teenage gang had started the trouble at the march. When King woke the next morning, three of the gang's leaders came to his hotel room and admitted that some of their members probably broke windows and threw rocks. They talked about how to put on a nonviolent march in Memphis, and King promised to include them in planning the next one. When they left, one of them called Dr. King an extraordinary man who would live up to his promises. King scheduled another demonstration for early April.

It rained heavily the night of Wednesday, April 3, when King returned to Memphis. Sick with a sore throat, he did not want to leave his room at the Lorraine Motel to go to the mass meeting at the Bishop Charles Mason Temple.

But after Ralph Abernathy called and urged him to come, he went.

Ralph gave Martin a long introduction, detailing his many accomplishments. The praise seemed to cheer Martin. Refreshed, he stepped up to the podium and said, "I know, somehow, that only when it is dark enough can you see the stars." While rain and thunder rattled the church windows, King spoke about hope. He said he was happy to live when oppressed people were fighting for freedom. He said he was happy he hadn't sneezed that night, years before, when he'd been stabbed and a sneeze would have killed him. He described threats against his life and said, "Like anybody, I would like to live a long life. Longevity has its place. But I'm not concerned about that now. I just want to do God's will." His voice lifted. He nearly sang. "I've *seen* the Promised Land. I may not get there with you. But I want you to know tonight, that we, as a people will get to the Promised Land. And I'm happy tonight. I'm not worried about anything. I'm not fearing any man. Mine eyes have seen the glory of the coming of the Lord." He stopped suddenly, seeming overcome with emotion, sweat and tears streaming down his face.

He slept until noon the next day, Thursday, April 4, and spent the early afternoon in meetings. Then he and his brother, A. D., called Mama King and spoke with her for nearly an hour. They were watching news on television when Andrew Young came in. Feeling jovial, King started hitting Young with a pillow. Pretty soon, the famous civil rights leaders were having an all-out pillow fight.

With Jesse Jackson *(left)* and Ralph Abernathy *(right)* at his sides, King stands on the balcony outside his room at the Lorraine Motel in Memphis, Tennessee. King returned to Memphis on April 3, 1968.

When they finally tired, King said everyone was invited to a soul food dinner at a friend's house.

It was nearly six o'clock in the evening. Martin and Ralph went upstairs to their room to dress. Martin shaved. Another friend came in and teased him about getting fat, as Martin searched for a shirt big enough to button easily. SCLC staff members milled in the parking lot downstairs, talking and shadowboxing. When Martin appeared on the balcony, his driver told him to get a jacket since it was getting cool. He went back inside, picked up his coat, then returned to the balcony.

King lies mortally wounded on the balcony outside his motel room on April 4, 1968. Jackson, Abernathy, and others point in the direction of the gunshot.

A loud, sharp bang burst, like a car backfiring. King fell and lay motionless. For a moment, his friends thought he was still joking. He wasn't. Ralph Abernathy was at Martin's side in an instant. He patted Martin's cheek and saw his eyes move. "Martin, Martin, this is Ralph. Do you hear me? Do you hear me?"

Martin was looking at Abernathy. He seemed to be trying to move his lips. But he couldn't say anything. Friends put a towel under his head and draped his body with a bedspread. Ralph kept talking to him until the ambulance came.

An hour later, at 7:05 P.M., the doctors at St. Joseph's Hospital in Memphis announced the death of the Reverend Dr. Martin Luther King Jr.

Afterword

The nation mourned Dr. King in many ways. When twelve-year-old Yoki learned about his death, she said, "My daddy . . . may be physically dead, but his spirit will never die." On Friday, April 5, President Johnson ordered flags flown at half-mast and declared Sunday, April 7, a national day of mourning. On Monday, April 8, Coretta Scott King and Ralph Abernathy led the peaceful march through Memphis that Martin had wanted. Yet at the same time, riots broke out in hundreds of cities across the country, killing forty-six people and injuring many thousands.

A recording of one of Martin's last sermons was played at his funeral on Tuesday, April 9. In the sermon, which he delivered at Ebenezer Baptist Church exactly one month before his death, he described what he wanted at his funeral. He said he didn't want his eulogy to mention his many awards or his fame. Instead, he wanted it said that he tried to love and serve humanity. A mule-drawn wagon, symbolizing conditions for the poor people of America, carried his casket to his grave. His tombstone bore the words he used to end his famous "I Have a Dream" speech: Free at last! Free at last! Thank God Almighty, I'm free at last!

Not long after the assassination, an escaped convict named James Earl Ray was arrested. He confessed to the killing. Although he later tried to withdraw his confession, he was convicted by a jury and went to prison. However, many people believed the FBI and the government conspired in the murder.

Less than two weeks after the assassination, the Memphis sanitation workers won their demands. The SCLC, led by Ralph Abernathy, decided to go ahead with the Poor People's Campaign. During May and June 1968, thousands of poor people camped in a shantytown called Resurrection City between the Lincoln Memorial and the Washington Monument in Washington, D.C. Heavy rainstorms turned the camp into mud, FBI and police undercover agents interfered, brawls and robberies plagued the residents, and squabbles among the SCLC leaders made many of their plans confused and ineffective. The campaign won a few, small victories, such as more money for government programs to feed poor people. Mostly, however, it ended in a slush of mud and disagreements.

Ten years later, in 1978, a congressional committee reviewed all of the evidence of King's assassination and decided Ray was indeed the murderer. He probably worked for a group of racists, including his family members, who thought segregationists would pay them a reward. Even so, theories about Ray's innocence and a government conspiracy remain. Ray died in prison in 1998.

A mural in Miami, Florida, honors the hope, passion, and work of Dr. Martin Luther King Jr. Other such monuments stand in cities across the United States. The nation celebrates his life each year with a national holiday on the third Monday in January.

In 1986 the third Monday in January was declared a national holiday in honor of Dr. King's birthday. Every year, television, radio, and news media carry stories about him, children study his speeches and his work, and offices and schools close to celebrate his life.

Great as he was, Martin Luther King Jr. was not perfect. He had faults and made mistakes. But he also had a conscience that led him to long for a better world, an imagination that helped him dream of one, and the determination to keep working for what he called the beloved community. The best way to achieve the beloved community, he taught, was to fight oppression with the powerful tools of love and nonviolent protest.

Dr. King was not the only one to teach this. Many people have struggled and suffered for justice. As Dr. King's SCLC colleague, Ella Baker, said, Martin did not make the civil rights movement—it made him. Still, his passion and his ability to communicate to masses of people thrust him into the forefront.

Together, Martin Luther King Jr. and the civil rights movement achieved great things and put a final end to Jim Crow segregation. But many of his dreams remain unfulfilled. Poverty, racism, injustice continue—and so do efforts to end them, as today's generations work to fulfill King's dreams.

The Civil Rights Act of 1964

P resident John F. Kennedy proposed the Civil Rights Act in 1963. After he was assassinated, Vice President Lyndon Baines Johnson became president and called for the law to be passed as a tribute to President Kennedy. Passing it was not easy. Some senators tried to talk it to death in a filibuster, a debate meant to keep a bill from becoming law. The debate went on for 75 days, one of the longest in Senate history. The bill passed anyway. President Johnson signed it on July 2, 1964, creating one of the most important civil rights laws in America.

However, the act left gaping holes. Its major achievement was desegregating most public businesses and services, such as hotels, restaurants and parks, but it allowed segregated private clubs without defining *private*. It encouraged public schools to integrate but did not authorize busing as a way to overcome school segregation. It outlawed job discrimination based on race but did not create a way to enforce that law. Most important, it outlawed racial discrimination in voter registration but still permitted literacy tests that prevented many African Americans from voting. Glad as he was that the Act passed, Martin Luther King Jr. knew plenty of work was still needed to achieve racial equality in America.

The following excerpt from the Civil Rights Act of 1964 deals with voting rights. It left so many loopholes that Congress had to pass another law the following year, the Voting Rights Act of 1965, to guarantee the right to vote to all citizens regardless of race.

Date: 02 JUL 64

88th Congress, H.R. 7152

An Act

To enforce the constitutional right to vote, to confer jurisdiction upon the district courts of the United States to provide injunctive relief against discrimination in public accommodations, to authorize the Attorney General to institute suits to protect constitutional rights in public facilities and public education, to extend the Commission on Civil Rights, to prevent discrimination in federally assisted programs, to establish a Commission on Equal Employment Opportunity, and for other purposes.

Be it enacted by the Senate and House of Representatives of the United States of America in Congress assembled, That this Act may be cited as the "Civil Rights Act of 1964."

TITLE I—VOTING RIGHTS

SEC. 101. No person acting under color of law shall—

(A) in determining whether any individual is qualified under State law or laws to vote in any Federal election, apply any standard, practice, or procedure different from the standards, practices, or procedures applied under such law or laws to other individuals within the same county, parish, or similar political subdivision who have been found by State officials to be qualified to vote;

(B) deny the right of any individual to vote in any Federal election because of an error or omission on any record or paper relating to any application, registration, or other act requisite to voting, if such error or omission is not material in determining whether such individual is qualified under State law to vote in such election; or

(C) employ any literacy test as a qualification for voting in any Federal election unless (i) such test is administered to each individual and is conducted wholly in writing, and (ii) a certified copy of the test and of the answers given by the individual is furnished to him within twenty-five days of the submission of his request made within the period of time during which records and papers are required to be retained and preserved pursuant to title III of the Civil Rights Act of 1960 (42 U.S.C. 1974—74e; 74 Stat. 88): Provided, however, That the Attorney General may enter into agreements with appropriate State or local authorities that preparation, conduct, and maintenance of such tests in accordance with the provisions of applicable State or local law, including such special provisions as are necessary in the preparation, conduct, and maintenance of such tests for persons who are blind or otherwise physically handicapped, meet the purposes of this subparagraph and constitute compliance therewith.

For the entire Civil Rights Act of 1964, visit *NARA: Digital Classroom* at <http://www.archives.gov/digital_classroom/lessons/civil_rights_ct/civil_rights_act.html>.

For a transcript of the Voting Rights Act of 1965, visit *Our Documents* at <http://www.ourdocuments.gov/doc.php?flash=true&doc=100&page=transcript>.

Browder v. Gayle: A Fight to Desegregate Montgomery Buses

On May 11, 1956, Claudette Colvin, a 15-year-old student at Booker T. Washington High School in Montgomery, Alabama, testified in court. During her testimony, she talked about being arrested for refusing to give her seat on a crowded bus to a white person and about her decision to boycott Montgomery buses. She was one of four women, called plaintiffs, who filed a lawsuit to have bus segregation in Montgomery declared illegal. The other three plaintiffs were Aurelia Browder, Susie McDonald, and Mary Louise Smith. They sued Montgomery mayor W. A. Gayle and others. The legal case was called *Browder v. Gayle*.

In her testimony, Colvin gave her name, address, and her parents' names. She said that before December 5, 1955—the start of the Montgomery bus boycott—she rode the buses twice a day. But on March 2, 1955, while on her way home from school at about 2:30 P.M. on the crowded Highland Gardens bus, the driver ordered her to stand up so a white person could sit down. She refused to give up her seat in the section of the bus designated for African Americans. According to the Montgomery segregation laws of 1955, African Americans did not have to give up seats in their section of buses if there were no other seat available. But the bus driver called the police anyway. Police came and arrested Colvin. This is part of her testimony from the *Browder v. Gayle* case.

> Claudette Colvin, called as a Witness, being duly sworn, testifies as follows:
>
> **COLVIN:** He [the bus driver] directly asked me to get up first. So I told him I was not going to get up. He said, "If you are not going to get up I will get a policeman. . . . He [policeman] said, "Why are you not going to get up?" He said, "It is against the law here." So I told him that I didn't know that it was a law. . . . I said I was just as good as any white person and I wasn't going to get up. . . . And then two more policemen came in. . . . So he [a police officer] asked me if I was going to get up. I said, "No, sir." I was crying then, I was very hurt because I didn't know that white people would act like that. . . . And he said, "I will have to take you off." So I didn't move. I didn't move at all. . . . So he kicked me and one [policeman] got one side of me and one [policeman] got on the other arm and they just drug me out. And so I was very pitiful. It really hurt me to see that I have to give a [white] person a seat, when all those colored people were standing and there were not any more vacant seats.

I had never seen nothing like that. Well, they take me down, they put me in a car and one of the [policemen], he says, "I am sorry to have to take you down like this." So they put handcuffs on me. . . .

[FRED] GRAY [plaintiffs' lawyer]: Where did they take you?

COLVIN: They take me to the City Hall. . . .

GRAY: Where did you go from City Hall?

COLVIN: I went to the City Jail. . . .

After Colvin described what happened at jail, Mayor Gayle's lawyer, Walter Knabe, asked whether Matin Luther King Jr. had influenced her to stop riding the buses.

KNABE: You have changed, that is, you and the other Negroes have changed your ideas since December 5, have you not?

COLVIN: No, sir. We haven't changed our ideas. It has been in me ever since I was born.

KNABE: But, the group stopped riding the busses for certain named things, that is correct, isn't it?

COLVIN: For what?

KNABE: For certain things that the Reverend King said were the things you objected to?

COLVIN: No, sir. It was in the beginning when they arrested me, when they [the African American community of Montgomery] seen how dirty they treated the Negro girls here, that they had began to feel like that all the time, though some of us just didn't have the guts to stand up.

KNABE: Did you have a leader when you started this bus boycott?

COLVIN: Did we have a leader? Our leaders is just we ourself.

Following Colvin's and and the other three women's stories of mistreatment and racism under Montgomery's bus system, the three judges hearing the *Browder v. Gayle* case overturned (reversed) the old court doctrine (a principle of law) that allowed "separate but equal" facilities for white people and black people. The doctrine of separate but equal came from a lawsuit in 1896 called *Plessy v. Ferguson,* in which U.S. Supreme Court justices held that racial segregation was legal. The court's decision in *Browder v. Gayle* was an early victory for the civil rights movement, challenging and defeating one aspect of nearly 60 years of legal segregation in the South.

Source Notes

7   Martin Luther King, Jr., *Testament of Hope: The Essential Writings and Speeches of Martin Luther King, Jr.* ed. James M. Washington (San Francisco: HarperCollins, 1991), 219.

9–10   Martin Luther King, Jr., in Clayborne Carson, ed., *The Autobiography of Martin Luther King, Jr.* (New York: Warner Books, 1998), 7–8.

10   Coretta Scott King, *My Life with Martin Luther King, Jr.,* (New York: Avon Books, 1970), 88.

15   Ibid., 93.

16   Martin Luther King, Jr., in *The Autobiography of Martin Luther King, Jr.,* 9.

17   Clayborne Carson, ed., *The Papers of Martin Luther King, Jr.* (Berkeley: University of California Press, 1992), 1:110.

19   Ibid., 112.

21   George D. Kelsey to Dean Charles E. Batten,.March 12, 1948, ibid., 155.

22   Charles E. Batten, "Confidential Evaluation of Martin Luther King, Jr.," February 23, 1951, ibid., 406.

23   Coretta Scott King, *My Life with Martin Luther King, Jr.,* 81.

25   Ibid., 108.

25   Martin Luther King, Jr., *Stride toward Freedom: The Montgomery Story* (New York: Harper and Row, 1958), 22.

28   Rosa Parks, *Rosa Parks: My Story* (New York: Dial Books, 1992), 115.

28   Ibid., 116.

31   Taylor Branch, *Parting the Waters: America in the King Years, 1954–63* (New York: Simon and Schuster, 1988), 138.

32   Clayborne Carson, ed., *The Papers of Martin Luther King, Jr.,* 1997, 3:71–74.

33   Branch, *Parting the Waters,* 149.

34   Martin Luther King, Jr., *Stride toward Freedom,* 129.

34   Ibid., 134–135.

37   Stewart Burns, *Daybreak of Freedom: The Montgomery Bus Boycott* (Chapel Hill: University of North Carolina Press, 1997), 72.

39   Martin Luther King, Jr., *Stride toward Freedom,* 173.

41   Burns, *Daybreak of Freedom,* 331–332.

42   Martin Luther King, Jr., *Stride toward Freedom,* 178.

42–43   David J. Garrow, *Bearing the Cross: Martin Luther King, Jr., and the Southern Christian Leadership Conference* (New York: Vintage Books, 1988), 89.

45   Carson, *The Papers of Martin Luther King, Jr.,* 2000, 4:210.

45   Ibid., 268.

47   Coretta Scott King, *My Life with Martin Luther King, Jr.,* 180.

48   Garrow, *Bearing the Cross,* 115.

48   Martin Luther King, Jr., *Testament of Hope,* 25.

51   Garrow, *Bearing the Cross,* 128.

53   Coretta Scott King, *My Life with Martin Luther King, Jr.,* 198–199.

57 Stewart Burns, *Social Movements of the 1960s: Searching for Democracy* (Boston: Twayne Publishers, 1990), 15.

58 David Wallechinsky, *The People's Almanac* (New York: Doubleday, 1975), 247.

59 Martin Luther King, Jr., *Why We Can't Wait* (New York: Signet Classic, 2000), 61–62.

61 Ibid., 60, 70.

64 Martin Luther King, Jr., *Testament of Hope,* 219.

68 David J. Garrow, *The FBI and Martin Luther King, Jr. (New York: Penguin Books,* 1983), 121–122.

69 David Lewis, *King: A Critical Biography* (New York: Praeger Publishers, 1970), 261.

69 Martin Luther King, Jr., *Testament of Hope,* 224–226.

71 Taylor Branch, *Pillar of Fire: America in the King Years, 1963–65* (New York: Simon and Schuster, 1998), 555.

71 Garrow, *Bearing the Cross,* 373.

71–72 Garrow, *Bearing the Cross,* 374.

72 Ibid., 376.

72 Ibid., 382–383.

73 Ibid., 386.

73 Ibid., 394.

74 Ellen Levine, *Freedom's Children: Young Civil Rights Activists Tell Their Own Stories* (New York: G. P. Putnam's Sons, 1993), 128.

75 Garrow, *Bearing the Cross,* 408.

79 Ibid., 439.

82 Martin Luther King, Jr., *Where Do We Go from Here: Chaos or Community?* (Boston: Beacon Press, 1967), 45–46.

85 Garrow, *Bearing the Cross,* 513.

86–87 *Eyes on the Prize,* vol. 5, VHS, directed by Callie Crossley, James A. Divenney, et al., (Milton, MA: Blackside/PBS Home Video, 1986).

87 Andrew Young, *An Easy Burden: The Civil Rights Movement and the Transformation of America* (New York: HarperCollins, 1996), 429.

88 Martin Luther King Jr., television interview by Arlene Francis, transcript, *Arlene Francis Show,* June 19, 1967, 6.

88–89 Martin Luther King Jr., "Doubts and Certainties," BBC interview, transcript, Martin Luther King Jr. Library, April 4, 1968, 9.

89 *Eyes on the Prize* 5.

92 Garrow, *Bearing the Cross,* 611–612.

94 Martin Luther King, Jr., *Testament of Hope,* 280, 286.

96 Young, *An Easy Burden,* 465–466.

97 Coretta Scott King, *My Life with Martin Luther King, Jr.,* 321.

103 *Browder v. Gayle,* 142 F. Supp. 707 (D.C. Ala. 1956), affirmed, 352 U.S. 903 (1956), in *Daybreak of Freedom,* Stewart Burns, ed. (Chapel Hill, NC: The University of North Carolina Press, 1997), 74–77.

Selected Bibliography

Branch, Taylor. *Parting the Waters: America in the King Years 1954–63.* New York: Simon and Schuster, 1988.

——. *Pillar of Fire: America in the King Years 1963–1965.* New York: Simon and Schuster, 1998.

Burns, Stewart. *Daybreak of Freedom: The Montgomery Bus Boycott.* Chapel Hill: University of North Carolina Press, 1997.

Carson, Clayborne, ed. *The Autobiography of Martin Luther King, Jr.* New York: Warner Books, 1998.

——. *The Papers of Martin Luther King, Jr.,* 4 vols. Berkeley: University of California Press, 1992–2000.

Dyson, Michael Eric. *I May Not Get There with You: The True Martin Luther King, Jr.* New York: Free Press, 2000.

Eyes on the Prize, VHS. 6 vols. Directed by Callie Crossley, James A. Divenney, et al. Milton, MA: Blackside/PBS Home Video, 1986–1987.

Garrow, David J. *Bearing the Cross: Martin Luther King, Jr., and the Southern Christian Leadership Conference.* New York: Vintage Books, 1988.

——. "King's Plagiarism: Imitation, Insecurity, and Transformation." *The Journal of American History,* June 1991.

King, Coretta Scott. *My Life with Martin Luther King, Jr.* New York: Avon Books, 1970.

King, Martin Luther, Jr. *Stride toward Freedom: The Montgomery Story.* New York: Harper and Row, 1958.

———. *Where Do We Go from Here: Chaos or Community?* Boston: Beacon Press, 1967.

———. *Why We Can't Wait.* New York: Signet Classic, 2000.

Lewis, David. *King: A Critical Biography.* New York: Praeger Publishers, 1970.

McKnight, Gerald D. *The Last Crusade: Martin Luther King, Jr., the FBI, and the Poor People's Campaign.* Boulder, CO: Westview Press, 1998.

Parks, Rosa. *Rosa Parks: My Story.* New York: Dial Books, 1992.

Ralph, James R. *Northern Protest: Martin Luther King, Jr., Chicago, and the Civil Rights Movement.* Cambridge, MA: Harvard University Press, 1993.

Robinson, Jo Ann Gibson. *The Montgomery Bus Boycott and the Women Who Started It: The Memoir of JoAnn Gibson Robinson.* Knoxville: The University of Tennessee Press, 1987.

Washington, James M., ed. *Testament of Hope: The Essential Writings and Speeches of Martin Luther King, Jr.* San Francisco: HarperCollins, 1991.

Young, Andrew. *An Easy Burden: The Civil Rights Movement and the Transformation of America.* New York: HarperCollins, 1996.

Other Resources

Books

Finlayson, Reggie. *We Shall Overcome: The History of the American Civil Rights Movement.* Minneapolis: Lerner Publications Company, 2003.

Greene, Meg. *Into the Land of Freedom: African Americans in Reconstruction.* Minneapolis: Lerner Publications Company, 2004.

Haskins, James. *Bayard Rustin: Behind the Scenes of the Civil Rights Movement.* New York: Hyperion, 1997.

Levine, Ellen. *Freedom's Children: Young Civil Rights Activists Tell Their Own Stories.* New York: G. P. Putnam's Sons, 1993.

Williams, Juan. *Eyes on the Prize: America's Civil Rights Years, 1954–1965.* New York: Penguin Books, 1988.

Videos

Boycott. DVD, based on *Daybreak of Freedom* by Stuart Burns. Directed by Clark Johnson. HBO Studios/Warner Home Video, 2002.

Mighty Times: The Legacy of Rosa Parks. VHS. Directed by Robert Houston. Montgomery, AL: Teaching Tolerance, Southern Poverty Law Center, 2002.

Websites

The King Center
<http://thekingcenter.org>
Visitors to the King Center website can find information about King, hear audio recordings of him, and access a timeline.

The Martin Luther King Jr. Papers Project at Stanford University
<http://www.stanford.edu/group/King>
This website offers access to the published papers and speeches of Martin Luther King Jr. Audio clips of some of King's speeches and sermons, as well as teachers' resources, are also available.

Index

The images in this book are used with the permission of: National Archives, pp. 1, 6 (background), 8 (background), 9 (background), 13, 17 (background), 26 (background), 40 (background), 49 (background), 58 (background), 64, 70 (background), 78 (background), 86 (background), 97 (background); © *Washington Post;* reprinted by permission of the D.C. Public Library, p. 2; Dictionary of American Portraits, p. 6; courtesy of the Library of Congress, pp. 8 (foreground) (LC-USZ62-125806 DLC), 14 (LC-USZ62-89701), 56 (LC-USZ62-118472); © Flip Schulke/ CORBIS, pp. 11, 21; Archives Collection, Birmingham Public Library, Birmingham, AL, pp. 18, 65; © Bettmann/CORBIS, pp. 24, 36, 39, 47, 60, 63, 75, 76, 83, 84, 90, 93; © Time Life Pictures/Getty Images, pp. 29, 33, 43, 44, 51, 54, 96; courtesy of the Lyndon B. Johnson Presidential Library, p. 66; © AP/Wide World, pp. 77, 95; League of Women Voters of Los Angeles Collection, California State University-Northridge, University Library's Urban Archives Center/photography by Los Angeles Fire Department, p. 79; © AFP/Getty Images, p. 87; © Getty Images, 99.

Cover: © *Washington Post*; reprinted by permission of the D.C. Public Library (foreground); National Archives (background).